SAINTS

SAINTS
A Visual Guide

Edward and Lorna Mornin

NOVALIS

Compilation © 2006 Frances Lincoln Ltd
Text © 2006 Edward and Lorna Mornin
All rights reserved

Published in Canada by

Novalis
10 Lower Spadina Avenue
Suite 400
Toronto, ON
M5V 2Z2
www.novalis.ca

First published 2006
in the United Kingdom by

Frances Lincoln Ltd
4 Torriano Mews
Torriano Avenue
London NW5 2RZ
www.franceslincoln.com

and in the United States of America by

Wm. B. Eerdmans Publishing Company
255 Jefferson Ave. S.E., Grand Rapids,
Michigan 49503 /
P.O. Box 163 Cambridge CB3 9PU U.K.
www.eerdmans.com

Manufactured in Singapore

Library and Archives Canada Cataloguing
in Publication: C2005-907245-8

10 09 08 07 06   5 4 3 2 1

ISBN: 2-89507-739-8

Half-title page: *The Four Gospel Writers*. Sgraffito
mural, 1961, by Georg Hahn. In the village of
Kreuth am Tegernsee, Bavaria.

Title page: *The Fourteen Holy Helpers*. Detail of
processional staff, 1998. Parish Church of
Eltmann, Bavaria.

CONTENTS

ACKNOWLEDGMENTS

The encouragement and material assistance of many people have furthered the composition of this book, and for this we thank them all. Herbert and Mathilde Seisenberger introduced us to the delights of rural churches in Upper Bavaria and accompanied us to visit many; Franz and Gabriele Mages did the same in Franconia. Volker Hoffmann provided us with scholarly perspectives on the saints. John Rengel retrieved information not easily accessible to us, and also provided the photographs on pages 158 and 171. Father Edward Kennedy's letter obtained access to buildings and spaces otherwise closed to the general public. William Mornin supplied us with timely and practical photographic advice and assistance. Marketa and Wladek Stankiewicz gave us constant encouragement, and a valued reference work. Marion Montgomery has permitted us to reprint her poem *Andrew*. Information on St Ninian was generously supplied by John Higgitt, while Edward Teixeira and Jo Beth Nolan conveyed their enthusiasm for St David and provided us with the photograph on page 172. At Frances Lincoln we would like to thank Jo Christian, Becky Clarke and Michael Brunstrom – and above all John Nicoll for his kindness and generosity and for placing his confidence in us to produce this book. Finally, our gratitude is due to all of those unnamed friends, colleagues, clergymen, church secretaries, and museum and church custodians who, in sharing their time, conversation, knowledge and passions with us, made the collecting of material for our project such a pleasure.

INTRODUCTION

Have you ever asked yourself who they are, those people represented in the statues, paintings or stained glass windows of churches? If you enjoy visiting churches, this must surely have been a frequent enough occurrence. You will doubtless have surmised that the figures generally depict saints, for at least a few of them are quite easily identifiable – Francis preaching to the birds, for example, or George with his dragon. Often the saint will be seen holding an object or in the presence of another person or an animal of presumably symbolic importance, or they may be shown in a particularly striking pose or attitude. Even when saints are named, as is usual in museums or art galleries, many questions will remain unanswered. Who were they when they were alive? Did they in fact exist, or were they as mythological as George's dragon? Why are they represented as they are? And what is the link between their lives or legends and their representation?

This book aims to answer some of these questions regarding the who, what, when, why, where and how of saints. Each entry contains a concise account of a saint's life or legend, highlighting the links between his or her story and representation. A typical portrayal of the saint or of the saint's symbol or attribute illustrates each text. A further important feature of the book is its key, designed to lead readers from particulars of a saint's representation to an identification and an explanation of the saint's emblems or signs. As the book's organization is broadly chronological, an index will direct readers to specific, known saints in whom they may be interested.

Directed at readers, religious or not, with a natural curiosity and an interest in the arts and in cultural history, religion, biography and legend, *Saints: A Visual Guide* includes more than 130 saints. This is, of course, far from an exhaustive listing. (*The Roman Martyrology*, the most comprehensive inventory, names some 4,500 saints.) As to the choice of examples, this is inevitably arbitrary, as a comparison between any two similar books will show all such undertakings to be. We have attempted, however, to be as representative as possible and to include as wide a range of the historically important Western saints as seemed feasible, contingent upon their being clearly enough identifiable in the first place. At the same time, we have felt no need to exclude historically unauthenticated saints such as Barbara or Margaret of Antioch. They are, after all, frequently seen in older churches, as well as in galleries and museums, and they are the focus of legends that, while entirely fictitious, are engaging in their own right and from a folkloristic viewpoint.

Over and above this, our selection of saints for treatment is frankly quite personal, though we hope not to have omitted too many of our readers' 'favourites'. C.P.S. Clarke, the author of *Everyman's Book of Saints*, comments on the problem of selection in his own inimitably English fashion: 'As in choosing a cricket eleven the first choices are easy and the last very difficult to make.' Our choice of examples reflects most clearly perhaps our own travels, in the course of which we only gradually developed the idea for a book by first attempting to answer our own questions about the saints we saw in churches and museums. Hence, Italy, Spain, southern Germany, Austria, France, Great Britain and the Americas have provided most of our illustrations – though it must be stressed that this is specifically a guide to saints, not to places. Personal quirks and predilections on the part of the authors, too, will no doubt be obvious enough, though these need scarcely concern us further here and will, one hopes, be viewed with indulgence.

Though dealing with the canonized, we have tried to avoid making our book too canonical in our choice of illustrations. Some of the world's foremost artists, especially up to the period of the Renaissance and again during the Counter-Reformation, have devoted some of their finest efforts to depicting saints. Such works are well represented in histories of art and receive their due in our book, too. We have not restricted ourselves to such classical portrayals, however, but have gone beyond these in order to look at a more eclectic range of images. We shall consider not only famous sculptures, paintings and engravings, but also more modest media, such as mass-produced church statuary, prayer cards, processional banners, commercial signs, and the like. Our conscious intention is to show the saints as we have encountered them, in a variety of formal and informal settings and not only as unique and awe-inspiring exhibits in churches, galleries or museums. At the same time, the iconographical principles underlying high art and popular or 'low' art are identical, and what matters for the practical purpose of identification is solely that a portrayal should be typical.

In its narrative sections, this book owes a great debt to the labour of other people, the (for us) most useful of whose works we include in our select bibliography. We have consulted many encyclopedias, dictionaries and 'books' of saints. Some of these, multi-volume compilations, constitute part of the classical corpus of saintly biography, legend and iconography; among these are the *Bibliotheca Sanctorum* (in Italian), *Ikonographie der Heiligen* and Butler's *Lives of the Saints*. Some single-volume works, too, have proved most helpful, including those by Farmer, Delaney, Attwater and Schauber/ Schindler. The classical source for accounts of early and medieval saints remains Jacobus de Voragine's thirteenth-century *Legenda Aurea*, which has been published in English numerous times, in whole or in part, as *The Golden Legend*. For a sifting out and elucidation of the historical, mythological and folkloristic components in the hagiographical tradition, it is unlikely that any work will ever excel Delehaye's *Legends of the Saints*. Yet even in these scholarly writings one encounters a good deal of divergence, and not a few contradictions and discrepancies, even occasional errors – for example, concerning dates, biographical particulars, details of legends, etc. This is not at all to be wondered at, but is rather in the very nature of any investigation into so many individuals, real, partly real or imaginary, from so many countries and different periods of history. We have made no great issue of such discrepancies. Given our goal, which is essentially a practical one, we have simply chosen what has seemed to us the most reliable (or, for a legend, the most traditional or widespread) version of a saint's life. At the same time, we hope ourselves in our rewriting not to have contributed further to new or extended versions of saintly lives or legends!

Almost unanimously, our friends in various countries have shown great enthusiasm for our work on the saints. Yet some, we must concede, have expressed surprise that we should devote ourselves to a study of this sort. The agnostics among them tend to wonder why one should bother at all with such superstitious vestiges of a bygone age. Our Protestant friends appear unsettled by the 'Catholic' character of our entire enterprise, forgetting perhaps that until the Reformation all of the saints were simply 'Christian'. Progressive Catholics, on the other hand, often enough wish to turn their backs on the picturesque past of wonders and miracles in order to focus exclusively on more contemporary religious role models they consider appropriate to our modern age (Mother Teresa of Calcutta or Archbishop Oscar Arnulfo Romero of San Salvador spring to mind). Confronted with such objections, one can argue that the saints of the past still merit attention today and are undeservedly neglected. They have, after all, given rise to some of the world's most sublime art, while their biographies and legends, though nowadays generally forgotten, are no less fascinating or entertaining on that account, and are often inspiring. Furthermore, the saints surround us in more ways than we sometimes imagine – not only in church decorations and church dedications, but also, for instance, in place names (San Francisco, São Paulo, the Saint Lawrence Seaway, the Court of St James, St Andrews Old Course) and in popular culture (Valentine cards, Catherine wheels, Santa Claus). Patron saints, too, are as much a part of national or popular cultures as of ecclesiastical observance, perhaps indeed more so. We are told that 'Frenchmen of all religious persuasions and none' (Dwyer) rejoiced at the canonization of Joan of Arc in 1920. Even if separated from the Emerald Isle by generations, Irish eyes surely still smile on St Patrick's Day. The image of St Christopher, patron saint of travellers, dangles from the key chain of many a godless motorist. In other words, the saints are simply too ubiquitous and too interesting to be granted as a monopoly to any one denomination or to the conventionally pious alone.[1]

It seems that at all times people have been remarkably ready to acknowledge the presence of saints around them – even that of saints who did not truly exist. Helen Roeder tells the amusing story of 'St Decimil'. A broken stone by the side of an old Roman road in Provence with the letters Decimil (Latin for 'ten thousand [paces]') was taken for the grave-marker of a saint rather than for the Roman milestone it in fact was. David Farmer informs us that the Scottish island of St Kilda does not commemorate a saint of that name, but probably represents a corruption of the Norse *skildir*, meaning 'shields', which was given to a group of small islands west of the Hebrides and was later transferred to the largest of them as St Kilda. Not even modern Americans are immune to the temptation of saint-making. Santa Nella in California does not commemorate a St Nell, but probably derives from the Spanish word *centinela* (sentinel), first given to a ranch and later to the modern community that stands on the same site. An entire dictionary, 1293 pages in length, has recently been devoted to fictitious saints in France and francophone Belgium alone. [2]

The question of what makes an individual a saint deserves some consideration here. (Let us hasten over Ambrose Bierce's definition, in his *Devil's Dictionary*, of a saint as a 'dead sinner revised and edited'.) In the earliest period of Christianity, saints were simply 'holy persons', acknowledged as such by popular acclaim. Hence Jesus's disciples (excluding Judas) and the gospel-writers were all held to be saints, as were also individuals close to or dear to him – his parents and grandparents and others such as Mary Magdalene or Joseph of Arimathea. To be put to death for one's Christian faith was seen from early times, and indeed continues to be seen today, as an imitation of Jesus's self-sacrifice on the cross and hence as a valid ground for sainthood. Various Roman emperors savagely persecuted and martyred Christians, so that Diocletian, who ruled from 284 to 305, is known as a veritable 'saint-maker'. Refusal to sacrifice to the Roman gods, one of whom after all was the emperor himself, was seen as an act of high treason. After the Emperor Constantine decreed religious tolerance for Christians throughout the Roman Empire in 313, however, various other ways to sainthood arose through other forms of self-sacrifice, or 'white martyrdom', as it has been called.

Such new routes to sanctity included living a life dedicated to God through the sacrifice of one's most basic creature comforts (as a hermit, for example) or of the consolation, pleasures or security of marriage through a vow of virginity or (for married persons, widows and widowers) of chastity. For this reason, as well as because the early Church generally considered sexuality acceptable only as a means of procreation and otherwise as base and degrading, virginity among saints has been, and within narrower limits continues to be, to the critical modern mind inordinately stressed. With the passage of time, however, a life of single-minded and selfless devotion to God, the Christian Church and Christian virtues emerged as the principal road to sainthood. To be sure, persons in religious orders, who no doubt possessed more talent, or opportunity, to dedicate themselves to such ends, most frequently attained this goal. At the same time, through the Christian belief in the communion of saints (articulated already in the fourth-century Apostles' Creed), saints could be invoked to intercede with God on one's behalf for the fulfilment of (worthy) wishes for oneself or others. Miracles, too, were from an early period ascribed to the intervention or intercession of the saints, and are still considered a requirement for canonization today. It should be noted, however, that miracles alone provide an insufficient basis for sainthood without proof (at least to the satisfaction of ecclesiastical investigators) of saintly character and of what the language of the Church terms 'heroic virtue'.

The declaration of an individual's sainthood was early considered the responsibility or prerogative of a bishop or diocese, and a saint's cult was centred on his or her tomb or mortal remains – gradually, however, also on other holy relics (such as a bone, an article of clothing or a possession) of the saint. Bishop Ambrose of Milan (a Doctor of the Church and himself later canonized) did much in the fourth century to establish veneration of the saints and their relics as standard practice. The possession of relics (or their acquisition, and hence dissemination, through purchase or gift) became the basis for the wealth, power, prestige and 'aura' of individual churches, monasteries and entire cities. From this derived the importance, for instance, of such great pilgrimage centres as Rome (relics of Peter, Paul, Laurence and many others), Cologne (relics of the Magi and Ursula), Compostela (relics of James Major) and Canterbury (relics of Thomas Becket).

Canonization (literally the entering of an individual's name in a 'canon', or list, of saints) was at the outset, then, a fairly informal procedure. Since, however, the naming of saints threatened with time to run out of control, responsibility for it was gradually vested in the papacy – the pope being considered a more objective and authoritative judge of sainthood than any mere bishop. Now a more rigorous investigation was conducted into the character and life of a candidate for sainthood, as well as into the nature and authenticity of his or her miracles, according at least to the science of the age. The first saint to be canonized by a pope was Ulrich in 993, and in 1234 the practice was made binding. The modalities of canonization were further refined, tightened and systematized at the Church Council of Trent (1545–63) and again in the seventeenth and eighteenth centuries. The most recent re-examination of the canonization process (and of the intermediate process of beatification, which precedes full canonization) came about through the Second Vatican Council (1962–5), resulting in a revision of the Roman calendar of saints in 1969.[3] As a consequence of this revision, certain well-known saints (for example, Margaret of Antioch and Catherine of Alexandria) were deleted from the calendar as spurious, while others (including George and Christopher) were reduced in status by being deemed worthy henceforth only of local veneration, no longer of universal veneration by the Church. At the same time, the revised calendar gives greater prominence to non-European saints and to those who were lay persons when alive. A similar change in emphasis is evident, too, in new canonizations today. These have not only been more numerous (the late John Paul II canonized more persons than all previous popes combined), but reflect the Church's present need for more non-European and lay saints. Such broadly 'political', and sometimes controversial, considerations have, to be sure, always been factors in the canonization process,[4] and influenced at the very least the timing of the canonization of such individuals as Joan of Arc and Bernadette of Lourdes.

Controversy of one sort or another is nothing new where the saints are concerned. Historically, it reached an early peak in Europe at the period of the Reformation in the sixteenth century. Reformers like Martin Luther assailed the veneration of saints and relics, like the sale of indulgences, as corrupt and as a theologically invalid means of courting divine favour. They wished to replace such outward observances as a means of obtaining grace with an emphasis on faith alone, to the exclusion even of good works. Lutherans, as well as Anglicans, and even some other denominations such as Presbyterians, have not entirely dispensed with saints, however. They have retained many of their old church dedications; and they continue even now to dedicate some new churches to them, at least to the more prominent among them such as the evangelists. Yet they create no new saints of their own.

Confounding what one might perhaps have expected, the post-Reformation Catholic Church did not downplay its saints. On the contrary, at the Counter-Reformation Council of Trent the validity of the cult of saints was reaffirmed. Furthermore, through the Council's emphasis on the worth of religious art as a reflection, however dim, of heavenly things, the building of churches and the portrayal of saints in sculpture and painting were enormously invigorated. This led to a flourishing of saintly iconography in the splendid Baroque abbeys and churches especially of Austria, Bavaria, Italy, Spain and Portugal (and also of Spanish and Portuguese possessions overseas). More modest churches, too, played an important part in this remarkable aesthetic renewal, which has still today not entirely spent its force. The results are evident in many rural and small-town parishes, as well as in cities, and not only in Catholic Europe, but also in many parts of North America and Latin America. That is what makes visiting churches, great and small, so rewarding. We hope that our book may enrich this experience for its readers or users by introducing them to new friends, as well as reacquainting them with old friends, among the saints that they encounter on their travels or through their reading.

---

[1] This book does not go into the matter of patronages in any detail, but mentions only the more important, interesting or unusual among them. Lists of patrons for countries, cities, trades and professions, as well as those saints to be invoked against various afflictions and in various situations, can be consulted, if need be, in several of the books listed in our bibliography.

[2] Jacques E. Merceron, *Dictionnaire thématique et géographique des saints imaginaires, facétieux et substitués en France et en Belgique francophone* (Editions du Seuil: Paris, 2002).

[3] Today's Roman calendar of saints is conveniently reproduced in John Delaney, *Dictionary of Saints* (Doubleday: New York, 1980), 622–38.

[4] For a discussion of past and especially present canonization procedures, including their political dimensions, see Kenneth L. Woodward, *Making Saints. How the Catholic Church Determines Who Becomes a Saint, Who Doesn't, and Why* (Simon and Schuster: New York, 1990).

THE SAINTS

ST MICHAEL

Actually, there lived no such person as Michael, for he is, with Gabriel and Raphael, one of the archangels named in the Bible. He is certainly a powerful entity. It was he who vanquished Satan and drove him out of heaven, and as such he is usually portrayed in armour trampling on or slaying a devil,

a dragon or a serpent. As a dragon slayer, he is clearly distinguishable from St George by his archangel's wings. As a guardian of the gates of heaven, he may be portrayed with a (sometimes flaming) sword and with scales with which to weigh the souls of the dead.

Michael is one of the most honoured of saints, and there are countless churches dedicated to him, often standing on high promontories, as at Mont-Saint-Michel in Normandy, or St Michael's Mount in Cornwall or in Le Puy, Auvergne. The main thoroughfare of the Latin Quarter in Paris is named for him – the Boulevard Saint-Michel, at the Seine end of which there stands, on the Place Saint-Michel, a huge monumental fountain dedicated to the archangel. Here he wields a sword and tramples a devil underfoot.

In Milton's *Paradise Lost*, God thus addresses Michael, the commander of the heavenly host, and his second-in-command Gabriel:

> Go, Michael, of celestial armies prince,
> And thou, in military prowess next,
> Gabriel; lead forth to battle these my sons
> Invincible; lead forth my armed saints
> By thousands and by millions ranged for fight.

Michael is, with George, a patron saint of soldiers, and also, amusingly, of grocers on account of the scales that he holds to weigh the souls of the dead.

Saint Michael Weighing Souls. Polychrome limestone, second half of fifteenth century, from the School of Maestro João Alonso of Coimbra. Museum of the Cathedral of Santiago de Compostela, Spain.

ST GABRIEL

Gabriel, like Michael and Raphael, was not a real person, but is one of the archangels mentioned in the Bible. It was he who announced to the Virgin Mary that she would give birth to Jesus. This scene, the Annunciation, has been much portrayed by Christian artists, perhaps most memorably by Fra Angelico. In his hand the winged Gabriel usually bears a lily, symbolic of Mary's purity – that is to say, of her birth without original sin (or immaculate conception). Because of his function as a bearer of messages, Gabriel was in 1921 declared the patron saint of the telephone, the telegraph and the post office.

As 'chief of th' angelic guards' of heaven, Gabriel, like the archangel Michael, figures prominently in Milton's *Paradise Lost*.

The Annunciation. Tempera on wood, 1430–32, by Fra Angelico. Museo del Prado, Madrid. Interestingly, there is no lily in this work. Fra Angelico alludes to original sin through the apple tree in the background and through Adam and Eve being driven out of Paradise.

ST RAPHAEL

Like Michael and Gabriel, Raphael is an archangel named in the Bible. More precisely, he occurs notably in the apocryphal Old Testament Book of Tobit. This is an account of the life of Tobit, supposedly written by Tobit himself, a pious Jew, at the behest of Raphael. Tobit had been blind, but through the intervention of the archangel his sight was miraculously restored by the medical application of the gall of a fish. (The name Raphael in Hebrew means 'God has healed'.) Raphael also cured the wife of Tobit's son Tobias of demonic possession through the use of the heart and lungs of the same fish. A major part of the Book of Tobit recounts a journey undertaken by Tobias in the company of the archangel and of a little dog.

Raphael is represented as a winged figure with a fish, sometimes accompanied by a young man (Tobias) and a dog, as in a celebrated fresco by Benozzo Gozzoli in the Church of Sant'Agostino in San Gimignano, Italy.

The city of San Rafael in California takes its name from its mission dedicated to the archangel. This mission was built by Spanish Franciscans as a hospital foundation in 1817 to care for sick Indians from the nearby mission of San Francisco, whose climate was considered less healthy.

St Raphael. Early painting, oil on canvas, by an unnamed California Indian from Mission San Luis Rey. Mission San Rafael, California.

ST ANNE

Anne was the mother of the Virgin Mary. No historical details are known about her life, however. Nor is she named or even mentioned in the Bible. She is first referred to in the apocryphal gospel of St James, dating from the second century. The enormous popularity of the Virgin in the European Middle Ages (in part a manifestation of the wider chivalric attitude towards women) led naturally enough to an interest in her parents, Anne and Joachim, and magnified their importance.

Today Anne is still one of the saints most frequently seen in churches. She appears as a mature woman in the company of the girl Mary, commonly in the charming situation of teaching her to read from a book. She is sometimes also depicted with Mary and the child Jesus (occasionally also with the child John the Baptist), or with her husband, Joachim.

In the New World, Anne (like Joseph, Mary's husband) enjoyed, and enjoys, particular veneration in Quebec. This reflects the importance of family values in the pioneering communities of early New France. The world's largest shrine to her is in Sainte-Anne-de-Beaupré, Quebec.

St Anne. Polychrome wood, attributed to Louis Jobin (1898–1928). Basilica Shrine of St Anne, Sainte-Anne-de-Beaupré, Quebec.

ST JOACHIM

Like St Anne, Joachim her husband is historically authentic
only to the extent that Mary, the mother of Jesus, must
certainly have had a father and a mother. There is no mention
of him in the Bible, and his name first occurs in a second-
century apocryphal text. According to this, he was a priest
who had had no children in twenty years of marriage with
Anne. Considered the result of some secret sin, their
childlessness became a cause for public reproach, so that the
high priest refused Joachim's sacrifice in the temple. Joachim
then withdrew in shame to his flocks in the wilderness,
whereupon an angel appeared to him and Anne announcing
the forthcoming birth of Mary.

Though a less popular saint than Anne, Joachim is
nevertheless quite frequently seen in her company in art, or,
alternatively, statues to each may stand on either side of a
church altar. Sometimes he appears simply as a long-bearded
older man, identifiable only through his proximity to Anne.
At other times he is shown as a shepherd, with a staff, or with
two doves or a lamb (referring to his rejected sacrifice).

St Joachim. Polychrome wood altar statue, 1862, by Anselm Sickinger.
Church of St Georg, Dinkelsbühl, Bavaria.

ST MARY

Of all the saints, Mary the mother of Jesus is the most universally and intensely revered. More churches are dedicated to her than to any other saint, as St Mary or as Our Lady (of Grace, of Mercy, of Perpetual Help, of the Sorrows, of the Sea, of the Snow, of the Portage, or of Fatima, of Lourdes, of Czestochova, of Guadalupe, of Walsingham, and so on).

Nothing is known of the historical Mary prior to her entry into the biblical narrative as the virgin chosen to bear God's son. Nor is anything of substance known about her life after the crucifixion, though both Jerusalem and Ephesus claim to be the place of her death, perhaps around the year 48. While she figures in art most familiarly holding the infant Jesus (Madonna) or with Joseph and the infant (Holy Family), she is portrayed also at other key points in the Bible story – for instance, at the annunciation (with Gabriel), the nativity, the flight into Egypt (with Joseph and the infant), the marriage at Cana, the crucifixion (with John the Apostle and Mary Magdalene) or the lamentation over the dead Christ (Pietà). A sword or seven swords, signifying her sorrows as the mother of Jesus, may pierce her breast. She is also frequently portrayed with other saints, such as her mother Anne or the boy John the Baptist, as well as with such historical figures as Bernadette of Lourdes. Occasionally she is seen protecting humanity (men, women and children) under her cloak.

In various parts of Europe in the past, a column might be erected to Mary to mark some momentous event, such as the end of a war or the passing of the plague. Such columns are particularly common in parts of Germany and Austria and may show her (as, for example, on the Marienplatz in Munich) as Mary the Immaculate, with a crown of stars, standing on the crescent moon and trampling on a serpent (symbolic of original sin). The belief in Mary's corporeal assumption into heaven (declared a dogma in 1950) and the subsequent coronation of the Virgin date from about the seventh century. These two scenes are frequently portrayed on Baroque altars or in the ceiling or cupola paintings of Baroque churches.

Our Lady as Protectress. Polychrome wood statue, 1489, by Peter Dell the Elder. Cathedral Museum, Fulda, Germany.

ST JOSEPH

Joseph was the husband of Mary, the mother of Jesus. Though supposedly descended from the royal house of David, he worked as a carpenter in Nazareth. He is mentioned at vital points in the early life of Jesus (for example, at the nativity and on the flight into Egypt), but nothing is known about his later life after Jesus began preaching.

Church statues often show this important saint as a bearded man with a lily (symbolic of purity), holding the infant Jesus or with the boy Jesus. Otherwise he is depicted with the tools of his trade, notably a square, a saw or a hammer.

Joseph is the patron saint of fathers, families, manual workers (especially carpenters) and of the entire Church. Like St Anne, he enjoys much popularity in Quebec, which boasts the world's largest shrine to him at St Joseph's Oratory in Montreal. No doubt to counteract the socialist tradition of May Day, the conservative Pope Pius XII in 1955 declared 1 May the feast of St Joseph the Worker.

Christ in the Carpenter's Shop. Oil on canvas, 1645, by Georges de La Tour. Musée du Louvre, Paris.

ST ELIZABETH

A significant figure in the Bible, Elizabeth was a kinswoman of the Virgin Mary and the mother of John the Baptist. Her story and that of her husband Zechariah, a priest, are related in Luke 1. Here the Archangel Gabriel appears to Zechariah in the temple and prophesies that his wife, though advanced in years and still childless, will give birth to a son whom they shall call John. The name in Hebrew means 'the Lord has been gracious'.

In the sixth month of Elizabeth's pregnancy, Mary, too, is visited by Gabriel. He announces that she will bear God's son, and informs her that Elizabeth, who has been thought barren, is expecting a child, for 'nothing is impossible with God'. Thereupon Mary pays a visit to her cousin in her native village. When Mary greets her, we are told, Elizabeth feels her child 'leap for joy' in her womb at the approach of the mother of the Lord. In an exchange between the two women, Elizabeth addresses Mary with the words: 'Blessed art thou among women, and blessed is the fruit of thy womb.' This salutation was later incorporated into the invocation and prayer of the 'Ave Maria' ('Hail Mary'). Mary replies with an expression of her joy that God has chosen a humble maiden like herself to bear his son. Her response evolved into the hymn of praise now called the 'Magnificat': *Magnificat anima mea Dominum*' ('My soul doth magnify the Lord'). The meeting between Elizabeth and Mary (known as the visitation) therefore provided important substance for the liturgy of the Church.

In art, Elizabeth characteristically appears as an elderly

woman standing together with the younger Mary. They may embrace or each place a hand on the other's womb, while Zechariah may also stand nearby.

The Visitation with Saints Nicholas and Anthony. On wood, 1489–90, by Piero di Cosimo. National Gallery of Art, Washington.

ST JOHN THE BAPTIST

John was Jesus's second cousin and only a little older than him. He lived as a hermit prophet in the wilderness calling on people to prepare themselves for the coming of the Messiah and to repent their sins, which he washed away through baptism. Jesus had himself baptized by John in the River Jordan, and John recognized him as the Messiah when he saw the Holy Spirit descend upon him in the form of a dove – a scene much depicted in art.

The Baptist provoked the anger of King Herod Antipas and Queen Herodias of Judea through denouncing their marriage as incestuous. (She was Herod's niece and had been married

to his half-brother.) Herodias's daughter Salome, to please her mother, danced for Herod for the reward of John's severed head (in the year 29 or 30).

John is usually represented as a bearded prophet dressed in animal skins, with a lamb and bearing in his hand a long cross to which may be attached a scroll with the words *'Ecce Agnus Dei'* ('Behold the Lamb of God'). This alludes to his recognition of Jesus as the Messiah who would be sacrificed to expiate the sins of others. He may point heavenwards, or to Jesus, or to the lamb.

The cruelty and eroticism of the Salome episode has appealed to many artists, including Caravaggio in his *Salome with the Head of St John the Baptist*. In 1893 Oscar Wilde wrote the French play that provided the (German) libretto for Richard Strauss's opera *Salome* (1905), in which John figures prominently.

John the Baptist Preaching. Fresco, 1732–3, by Giovanni Battista Tiepolo. Cappella Colleoni, Bergamo, Italy.

ST ANDREW

Andrew, a fisherman like his younger brother Peter, was the first disciple that Jesus called to him. He is mentioned at various points in the scriptures, notably for his part in the feeding of the five thousand. Like the other disciples, Andrew after the crucifixion undertook missionary journeys – in his case at least to Greece, for it was in Patras, Greece, that he was martyred around the year 60.

Andrew is usually portrayed as white-haired and bearded, with his symbol of a diagonal cross. Legend has it that he was crucified on such a cross, though this tradition dates from no earlier than the tenth century. Another unfounded tradition relates that his relics were brought in the fourth century to

Scotland, where they became an important destination for pilgrims in the town later called St Andrews (better known today as a mecca for golfers). A white diagonal cross on a blue ground is the national flag of Scotland, whose patron Andrew is.

For St Andrew's Day (30 November) in the millennial year 2000, *The Glasgow Herald* published the following poem, showing how old saints may still have something of substance to say in today's world.

Andrew

Why me? You Scots shuid hae a sodger saint
Like George the dragon-slayer.
Or if ye maun choose frae the Twelve
Tak James or John, the sons of thunder, fierce
Agin auld neebor foe, Samaria,
Or zealot Simon wantin shot o Rome.
Thomas wi his doubts, or speirin Philip
Wid suit ye better nor a fisher lad
Wha didnae argue or ding sinners doon,
Jist listened and ca'd ither fowk tae hear.
But some chiel brought my banes tae this grey shore.
Its kirk in ruins and its harbour silted,
Whaur can I cast my net for fish or men?
Syne I must stand for Scotland,
Please God she too will share her loaves
And fishes wi the lave and keep an open mind.

Marion Montgomery

Saint Andrew and Saint Francis. Oil on canvas, 1595, by El Greco.
Museo del Prado, Madrid.

ST PETER

Peter was the most forceful of Jesus's disciples and played a dominant part in the emergence of the Christian Church. Like his brother Andrew, he was a fisherman before Jesus made them 'fishers of men'. His original name was Simon, but Jesus called him Peter – in Greek *petros,* meaning stone or rock. Artists have illustrated many of the scenes in which he figures in the Bible – for instance, casting his nets, walking on the Sea of Galilee, cutting off the ear of a servant of the high priest, or denying Jesus before the cock crows. After the crucifixion he preached in various parts of the Roman Empire, including Rome itself. Here he was crucified under the Emperor Nero about the year 65 – it is said upside down, because he claimed to be unworthy of being crucified in the same way as Jesus. The scene is depicted by Michelangelo in his fresco of the *Martyrdom of St Peter* in the Cappella Paolina in the Vatican. The saint's tomb can be visited today in the crypt of St Peter's Basilica in Rome.

Technically the first Bishop of Rome, Peter was therefore also the first Pope. His ultimate authority, and the authority of popes for Catholics ever since, rest on the passage in Matthew 16: 18–19: 'And I say unto thee that thou art Peter, and upon this rock I will build my church; and the gates of hell shall not prevail against it. And I will give unto thee the keys of the kingdom of heaven.'

Peter is most often portrayed as an older, bearded man carrying keys, and sometimes standing on a rock. Keys are also the symbol of the papacy, to be seen in the papal arms and on the papal flag. Another of his emblems is the rooster, both signifying vigilance and referring to his denial of Jesus. He may also be shown as a fisherman.

St Peter. Polychrome wood altar statue, *c.* 1625, by Philipp Dirr. Cathedral of St Maria and St Korbinian, Freising, Bavaria.

ST JOHN THE APOSTLE

The brother of James Major and the youngest of the twelve disciples, John is traditionally identified as the unnamed 'disciple whom Jesus loved' and to whom from the cross he confided the care of his mother. He was the only disciple present at the crucifixion. After Jesus's death, he was prominent in the formation of the early Christian Church in Jerusalem and in Asia Minor, where he settled at Ephesus. For a time he associated closely with Peter. Having survived persecution (the only disciple to do so), he died at an advanced age, probably in Ephesus, around the end of the first century. He was most likely the author of the fourth gospel, but only reputedly of the Book of Revelation (Apocalypse), which tradition claims he wrote on the Mediterranean island of Patmos, to which he was for a time exiled.

In art John is characteristically depicted as a young, usually beardless, man with long hair. He figures in many scenes of the crucifixion, together with (and sometimes supporting) Jesus's mother. In other portrayals, he is shown holding a book (his gospel), while as an evangelist he is symbolized by the eagle, because of the soaring, sublime style of his writing. (For the same reason he is also known as John the Divine.) A legend tells how he miraculously survived drinking a cup of poison given to him by a pagan priest of Ephesus. This is sometimes commemorated, as for example in El Greco's *St John the Evangelist,* by depicting John holding a goblet from which a snake, or a little dragon, rears its head.

Saint John the Apostle. Marble relief, early sixteenth century,
by Vasco de la Zarza. Ávila Cathedral, Spain.

ST JAMES MAJOR

James, like his brother John the Apostle, was a disciple of Jesus, who called the two the 'sons of thunder' on account of their fiery temperament. Because, along with Peter and John, he enjoyed a certain pre-eminence among the disciples (or perhaps simply because he was older or taller), he is termed Major (or the Great) to distinguish him from the other disciple James (Minor, or the Less). James Major was the first disciple to be martyred for his faith, being put to the sword in Judea in the year 44.

Various legends generally accorded little credence outside of Spain link him with that country, whose patron he is. It is claimed even that he preached and died there. Certainly, the church of Santiago (St James) de Compostela in Galicia, north-west Spain, claims his relics. These made Compostela one of the prime destinations of European pilgrimages in the Middle Ages. Because Compostela lies near the Atlantic, it was customary for pilgrims to display a scallop shell from the shore to show that they had been there. Statues to James or inns named after him are still common along the pilgrim routes to Compostela today, and Compostela remains an important goal for pilgrims, as well as for hikers and cyclists. The name Compostela itself debatably derives from Giacomopostolo (James the Apostle).

James is commonly represented as a pilgrim with a wide-brimmed hat, displaying a scallop shell and holding in his hand a knobbed pilgrim's staff, perhaps with a gourd water bottle attached. Somewhat paradoxically, then, he is seen as a pilgrim returning from his own shrine. Artists including Tiepolo have portrayed the saint on horseback slaying Moors (in Spanish, *Santiago Matamoros*), reflecting the story of James's miraculous appearance to assist the Christians against the Moslems in the Battle of Clavijo in 844.

Coquilles St Jacques (St James scallops) is a seafood specialty one can find on the menu of many a good French restaurant.

Chaucer's Wife of Bath in his *Canterbury Tales* had visited Compostela as well as other notable pilgrimage centres:

And threis hadde she been at Jerusalem:
She hadde passed many a strange stream;
At Rome she hadde been, and at Boloigne,
In Galice at Seint-Jame, and at Coloigne.

St James. Polychrome wood statue, fourteenth century, restored 2000.
Royal Collegiate Church of Roncesvalles, Spain.

ST MATTHEW

The alleged author of the first gospel (though probably the second to be composed), Matthew belonged to a class of persons much despised in his age, for before being called by Jesus he was a publican, a Jewish tax-collector for the Romans. Little is known about what happened to him after the crucifixion, though tradition has it that he preached in Judea and Persia, where he was perhaps martyred around 74.

As an evangelist, Matthew carries a book (his gospel). He is symbolically accompanied by a (sometimes winged) man (who may be mistaken for an angel), because his gospel stresses Jesus's human ties, opening as it does with an account of his genealogy and descent from King David. Otherwise he is depicted holding the assumed instrument of his martyrdom (a spear, a sword or a halberd) or with a money bag or a money box recalling his earlier profession as a tax-gatherer. He appears in this latter guise, for example, in paintings of *The Calling of St Matthew* by Carpaccio and by Caravaggio.

The Inspiration of Saint Matthew. Oil on canvas, 1602, by Caravaggio. Cappella Contarelli, Church of San Luigi dei Francesi, Rome.

ST JAMES MINOR

James Minor was possibly a relative of Jesus and, like James Major, was one of the twelve disciples. Though there is some uncertainty about his identity, it was probably he who after the crucifixion became the leader of the Jewish Christian Church in Jerusalem. This would have made him one of the most influential figures in the early Church. He is said to have been martyred in the year 62 by being thrown from the walls of the temple in Jerusalem and then bludgeoned to death with a fuller's club.

James is recognizable by his emblem of a fuller's club, which looks rather like a long bow.

St James Minor. Wood engraving, *c.*1516–19, by Hans Baldung Grien.

ST THOMAS

Thomas, one of the twelve disciples, is popularly known as 'doubting Thomas'. It was he who asked for proof of the corporeal reality of the risen Christ and who would not believe until he himself had touched Jesus's wounds. After the crucifixion, like the other disciples, Thomas probably travelled preaching the word, though no certain details are known about his journeys. There is a strong tradition, however, that he preached in southern India, where he is supposed to have been martyred at Mylapore, near Madras, around the year 72.

Many painters have depicted the scene of Thomas touching the wound in Jesus's side. Otherwise, the saint is shown bearing either a spear (the supposed instrument of his martyrdom) or a builder's square, because he is said to have built a palace for an Indian prince. He holds a square, for instance, in Le Gros's monumental statue of St Thomas in St John Lateran, Rome. For this reason, too, he is the patron saint of architects.

Doubting Thomas. Tempera on wood, 1308–11, by Duccio.
Museo dell'Opera del Duomo, Siena.

ST BARTHOLOMEW

Bartholomew, one of Jesus's twelve disciples, is so called in the first three gospels, while the fourth gospel names him Nathaniel. Nothing definite is known about his life after the crucifixion. Tradition relates, however, that he preached in India and Armenia, where he was reputedly martyred by being flayed alive.

The savage martyrdom of Bartholomew has appealed to the imagination of many artists, who portray him being flayed, or as a disciple in long robes holding a flaying knife, sometimes with his own skin draped over his arm. Paradoxically, he is the patron saint of tanners and of others who work in skins or hides.

A negative connotation attaches to St Bartholomew in France, for it was on his feast day (24 August) in 1572 that many thousands of Protestant Huguenots were massacred at the command of Catherine de Médicis.

Saint Agnes, Saint Bartholomew and Saint Cecilia. On wood (undated), by the Master of the St Bartholomew Altar. Alte Pinakothek, Munich.

ST PHILIP

Philip was a fisherman before being called by Jesus to be his disciple. Not unlike Thomas, he is considered a rather literal-minded or 'questioning' individual, seeing, for instance, the feeding of the five thousand primarily in a financial or logistical light. Nothing definite is known about his life after the crucifixion, though tradition relates that he preached in Greece and that he also died a martyr's death there at Heliopolis, Phrygia (in today's Turkey). The church of Santi Dodici Apostoli (the Twelve Apostles) in Rome claims his tomb, though the claim is contested.

Among the disciples, Philip is usually identifiable by the long cross that he carries as the possible instrument of his martyrdom. He may also appear with a dragon, as *The Golden Legend* relates that he vanquished such a creature.

St Philip. Marble statue, 1703–12, by Giuseppe Mazzuoli.
Basilica of St John Lateran, Rome.

ST SIMON

Simon was one of Jesus's twelve disciples and was possibly related to him. As he is sometimes called Simon the Zealot, one assumes he belonged to the Zealots, the Jewish resistance group that then opposed the Roman presence in Judea. After the crucifixion he is said to have preached together with his brother St Jude in Persia, where they are supposed to have been martyred. Reputedly Simon was sawn in half.

Among the disciples, Simon can be recognized by his emblem of a long saw.

St Simon. Marble statue, 1708–9, by Francesco Moratti.
Basilica of St John Lateran, Rome.

ST JUDE (or THADDEUS)

Jude (not to be mistaken for Judas) was possibly a relative of Jesus. One of the twelve disciples, he is named Jude by Luke in the Acts of the Apostles, and he is usually identified with the apostle called Thaddeus by Matthew and Mark. Tradition relates that after the crucifixion he preached in Persia together with his brother the apostle Simon. Here, too, both men were martyred.

In representations Jude characteristically carries a club (or, frequently in Spain, an axe) as the supposed instrument of his martyrdom. He may also display a picture of Jesus, in reference to a legend that Jesus impressed his image on a piece of cloth with which Jude cured the king of Edessa in Mesopotamia of leprosy, resulting in mass conversions among his people.

Probably because he is easily confused with Judas, people have assumed that one should turn to Jude to intercede for them only when all else fails, for which reason he has become known as the patron saint of 'lost causes'. This has by no means diminished his popularity, however, as is proved by the frequency of statues to him in churches today.

St Jude. Plaster statue, *c.* 1970.
Church of Sts Peter and Paul, San Francisco, California.

ST MATTHIAS

Matthias is mentioned only once in scripture (Acts 1: 21–26), where he is named as the disciple chosen by lot by the apostles to replace the traitor Judas. Nothing of certainty is known about his later life, though legend claims that he preached in Judea, Asia Minor and the area of the Caspian Sea, where he is said to have been martyred.

There has been some confusion between Matthias and Matthew due to the similarity of their names. Among the apostles, he is usually recognizable by his emblem, an axe or a halberd, as the possible instrument of his martyrdom.

St Matthias. Polychome wood statue, 1696, by Georg Pämer.
Parish Church of Mariä Himmelfahrt,
Grassau, Chiemgau, Bavaria.

ST MARY MAGDALENE

Mary Magdalene, so called after her native village of Magdala near the Sea of Galilee, is familiar from the gospels as a woman follower of Jesus. She is considered the archetypal repentant sinner, her story having been conflated with that of the (unnamed) immoral woman who washed Jesus's feet with her tears, dried them with her hair and anointed them with myrrh, and whom Jesus pardoned. Similarly, she is often confused with Mary of Bethany (the sister of Martha and Lazarus), who also anointed Jesus's feet and dried them with her hair. Luke specifically names Mary Magdalene as having had devils cast out of her by Jesus. She was also a central figure at the crucifixion and resurrection: she stood at the foot of the cross, was prepared to anoint Jesus's body for the tomb, discovered the empty tomb on Easter morning, and was the first to see him after he left the tomb. A common tradition says that after these events she went to the south of France, together with Martha and Lazarus – again an evident conflation with Mary of Bethany. Several sites in France claim to possess her relics.

The patron saint of hairdressers, Mary Magdalene is readily identifiable in art by her long flowing hair, with which she supposedly dried Jesus's feet. She often holds a pot of ointment to anoint his feet or prepare his body for burial. So she appears in Raphael's *Saint Cecilia* (see page 100). She may also be shown with a skull – that is, as a penitent contemplating the transience of worldly vanities. Often she is shown at the crucifixion, and hence on occasion with the instruments of the crucifixion.

Saint Mary Magdalene. Oil on canvas, 1623–7, by Simon Vouet.
Galleria Nazionale d'Arte Antica, Rome.

ST MARTHA

The gospels of Luke and John relate how Jesus visited the home of Martha and of her brother Lazarus and sister Mary at Bethany. On this occasion Jesus chided Martha for her complaint that Mary did not help sufficiently with the household chores for his visit. This is generally regarded as an endorsement of the value of a life of adoration and contemplation of Jesus as distinct from a life of merely worldly concern. At the same time, Martha is recognized for the value of her practical work in assisting the mission of Jesus.

Martha, the patron saint of housewives and lay sisters, is represented as a housewife in homely attire, perhaps with a basket or keys, a ladle or a broom.

St Martha. Polychrome wood statue. Church of Santa Cruz, Madrid.

ST LAZARUS

One quite frequently sees representations of Lazarus today, particularly on prayer cards for private devotions, a popularity perhaps ascribable to the fact that he is invoked by or for the terminally ill – surely a relatively unchanging proportion of any population. Lazarus appears in the Bible (John 11: 1–44) as the brother of Martha and Mary of Bethany and the friend of Jesus, who raises him from the dead in his most dramatic miracle. An eleventh-century legend relates that Lazarus left Palestine with his sisters and Mary Magdalene and came by boat to the south of France, where they made many converts and where he is supposed to have become the first Bishop of Marseilles.

Lazarus of Bethany, however, has become conflated with that other Lazarus of the parable in Luke (16: 19–31), a diseased and dying beggar who lies at the door of a rich man in the hope of obtaining his charity. So miserable is Lazarus's state that the dogs lick his sores.

St Lazarus is portrayed as a wretched beggar with sores, supporting himself on a crutch and followed by dogs.

A lazar house, or lazaretto, was a house for 'lazars', persons afflicted by loathsome diseases such as leprosy or the plague. A congregation of Lazarists, founded by Vincent de Paul in 1625, took its name from the Paris priory of Saint Lazare, which was its headquarters. Saint Lazare railway station in Paris was the earliest to be built in the city.

St Lazarus. Printed prayer card from Italy.

ST VERONICA

Veronica was reputedly a matron of Jerusalem who stood by the wayside to watch Jesus pass on his way to Calvary. Moved to compassion when he fell under the weight of his cross, she wiped the sweat from his brow with her head-cloth. According to one of her many legends, this left the imprint of his visage on her cloth. It is commonly supposed that this story derives from a pun on the name Veronica, which suggests *vera icon* (true image). Nothing is known about a historical Veronica, and though she is a well known figure in art she is not listed in the *Roman Martyrology*, the definitive listing of Christian saints. Artists represent her as a woman holding a cloth bearing the image of Jesus's face. She can be seen at the sixth of the fourteen stations of the cross in Catholic churches.

In Spanish bullfighting one of the classic movements with the cloak is called the *veronica*. In it the matador must pass his cloak in front of the bull's horns so slowly that it resembles Veronica wiping Jesus's brow.

Saint Veronica Holding the Veil. Oil on canvas, *c.* 1580, by El Greco. Museo de Santa Cruz, Toledo, Spain.

ST STEPHEN

Stephen is known as the 'protomartyr' because he was the first Christian to be killed for his faith. His story is told in the Acts of the Apostles 6–7. He was a deacon and a leader of the group of christianized Jews resident in Jerusalem after the crucifixion. Arrested for blasphemy, he was tried by the Jewish Sanhedrin court, from where, despite an eloquent self-defence, he was dragged to the outskirts of the city and stoned to death. This happened in the year 35.

Stephen is represented as a young and beardless man holding stones. On the assumption that being struck on the head with a stone killed him, he is invoked against headaches.

Because of his status as the earliest martyr, St Stephen's Day (26 December) appropriately follows immediately upon Christmas Day. It is referred to in the familiar Christmas carol:

Good King Wenceslas looked out
On the feast of Stephen,
When the snow lay round about
Deep and crisp and even.

St Stephen. Plaster statue. Basilica of San Lorenzo fuori le Mura, Rome.

ST PAUL

Paul, whose original name was Saul, was born a Jew in Tarsus, in today's Turkey, sometime between the years 5 and 15. He never knew Jesus personally, and actually took an active part in the early persecution of the Church. However, when on the road from Jerusalem to Damascus to take custody of some Christian prisoners, he experienced an intense vision of Jesus that resulted in his dramatic conversion. Artists have portrayed this scene as Paul being struck from his horse by a bolt of lightning or a ray of light.

Paul is known as the Apostle of the Gentiles because it was he, often against considerable opposition, who first carried the gospel to non-Jews. Hence, he contributed perhaps more than any other individual to the spread of the Christian Church as it exists today. He was a tireless worker, an inspired preacher, and a brilliant organizer whose letters to the young Christian churches constitute a considerable part of the New Testament. His missionary journeys took him to many parts of the Roman world, from Palestine perhaps even as far as Spain. In Rome he associated closely with Peter, and it was here around the year 65 that he was beheaded under the Emperor Nero. Over his tomb was built the church of San Paolo fuori le Mura (St Paul's Outside the Walls) in Rome.

In art Paul is represented as dark-haired and fiery-eyed, bearing a lowered sword (as the instrument of his martyrdom or the symbol of his activism) and sometimes carrying a book or his epistles. This is how he appears in Raphael's painting of Cecilia (see page 100). He is often seen in the company of

Peter, for instance on church altars, or as one of the twelve apostles (where he may replace Matthias). Not infrequently, churches have a dual dedication to Sts Peter and Paul.

St Paul. Tapestry, twentieth century. Church of St Paul, Munich.

Saint Mark the Evangelist. Fresco, 1486–90, by Domenico Ghirlandaio.
Cappella Tornabuoni, Santa Maria Novella, Florence.

ST MARK

Mark, the author of the second gospel (actually the first to be completed), probably never met Jesus, but knew both Paul and Peter, and it was on Peter's teachings and testimony that his gospel was largely founded. One of the first generation of Christians, Mark made missionary journeys to various parts of the Mediterranean world, including Egypt, Cyprus and Italy, where he may have composed his gospel in Rome sometime between the years 65 and 70. He died in Alexandria, Egypt, around 74. His body was brought to Venice in 829 and rests today in the church of San Marco in Venice, whose patron he is.

Mark's symbol as an evangelist is a (sometimes winged) lion. In art he is represented with his gospels and with, or sometimes by, a lion. The lion emblem is much in evidence in Venice. There is no unambiguously clear link between Mark's life or gospel and his emblem, however. It is frequently pointed out that his gospel opens with John the Baptist preaching in the wilderness, the habitat of lions. C.P.S. Clarke suggests a basis for the emblem in an ancient superstition that a lion is born dead and is only aroused to life on the third day by the bellowing of its sire. This would correspond to Mark's emphasis on the story of the resurrection, with which his gospel closes.

ST LUKE

As the author of the third gospel and also of the Acts of the Apostles, Luke played a vital part in the transmission of the gospel story and of the history of the early Church. Most likely of Greek descent, he was probably born in Antioch, in present day Turkey, around the beginning of the Christian era. He was a physician by profession.

Though he never met Jesus, Luke was close to people who had known him personally, and he was among the earliest converts, perhaps through St Paul. He accompanied Paul for some years on missionary journeys and spent time with him in Philippi (Greece), Rome and Jerusalem. According to tradition, he died a peaceful death at the age of eighty-four.

Luke's gospel is generally judged the most literary and poetic of the four, and as an 'artist in words', he was adopted as the patron saint of the medieval artists' guilds and is the patron of artists (painters). Unfounded tradition claims that he himself was an artist and painted a portrait of the Virgin Mary – a subject of many works, for example by Guercino, Heemskerck and Jan Gossaert. As a physician, he is also a patron saint of doctors and surgeons.

In art Luke carries a book (his gospels) and is usually accompanied by an ox (sometimes winged), which is his emblem. The reason for this remains obscure, though some suppose that the ox, as a common sacrificial animal, suggests the element of sacrifice that Luke stresses in his gospel.

Saint Luke. Marble relief, early sixteenth century, by Vasco de la Zarza.
Ávila Cathedral, Spain.

The Martyrdom of Saint Clement. Oil on poplar wood, *c.* 1500,
by Bernardino Fungai. York Art Gallery.

ST CLEMENT

Tradition claims that Clement was born a Jew in Rome and was baptized by St Peter himself. Certainly, he was the fourth pope, acceding to the papal throne in the year 91. As a result of the extent and vigour of his proselytizing activities as pope, he was exiled from Rome to the Crimea by the Emperor Trajan. Even in exile, however, he continued to propagate the faith so zealously that he was martyred in the year 100. Legend relates that he was thrown into the sea with an anchor around his neck and that angels built him a tomb on the sea floor.

Clement is represented as a pope with an anchor, recalling his martyrdom. His name is familiar to all through the nursery rhyme:

Oranges and lemons,
Say the bells of St Clement's.
You owe me five farthings,
Say the bells of St Martin's.

The reference here is to the church bells of St Clement Danes in London's Strand and of St Martin in the Fields on today's Trafalgar Square.

ST EUSTACE & ST HUBERT

Separated as their lives were by some six centuries, Eustace and Hubert may at first seem unlikely candidates for joint treatment. Yet their legendary lives so closely resemble each other that their emblematical presentations are virtually indistinguishable.

Eustace (Latin: Eustachius) is a saint of uncertain date and doubtful authenticity whose cult was suppressed in 1969. According to legend, he had been a Roman general under the second-century Emperor Trajan and was converted to Christianity when he encountered a stag with a crucifix between its antlers. He and his family, who also converted, were martyred by being burnt alive for refusing to sacrifice to the Roman gods. He is one of the (relatively less well known) Fourteen Holy Helpers.

Hubert certainly was a historical figure. He was a bishop of Maastricht (in today's Netherlands) and Liège (in today's Belgium) who died in 727. Little is known about his early life, and his legend did not originate until the fourteenth century, its salient features being borrowed from the story of Eustace. According to his legend, Hubert was a worldly man much given to hunting until one Good Friday, when, hunting instead of attending church, he beheld a vision of the crucified Christ between the antlers of a stag. This resulted in his conversion to religion and in his future ecclesiastical career.

Each of these saints is portrayed as a hunter in the presence of a stag with a cross between its antlers. Not surprisingly,

they are patron saints of hunters. Shrines to the saint with the stag and crucifix can be commonly seen in some rural and wooded areas of Catholic Europe.

Vision of Saint Eustace. Tempera on wood, *c.* 1435, by Pisanello.
National Gallery, London.

ST URBAN

Urban I was an early pope who died in Rome in the year 230 and about whose life barely anything is known with historical certainty. What perhaps matters most about him today is that his feast day (the anniversary of his death) falls on 25 May. This is the date by which German vintners, it is claimed, must have completed all preparatory work in their vineyards for the new growing season.

Urban is the patron saint of vintners and hence is especially popular in wine districts of Europe such as Franconia, Baden and Alsace. He is represented as a pope, or sometimes as a bishop, bearing a bunch of grapes.

St Urban. Devotional statuette in shop window, Oberammergau, Bavaria.

ST DENIS

A native of Italy, Denis (Latin: Dionysius) was sent with five or six other bishops to convert Gaul around 250. He preached with great success and founded a centre of Christian worship at Paris, whose first bishop he became. Around 258, on the hill now known as Montmartre (Martyrs' Hill), he and two companions were beheaded by one of the local pagan chieftains. Over their tombs was later built the abbey church of Saint-Denis (on the outskirts of present day Paris), which became the burial place of French kings.

Legend has it that Denis walked from his execution to his grave with his head in his hands. This story perhaps arose from an old painting in which the artist placed the saint's mitred head in his hands so that his body could be identified. He is portrayed as a bishop carrying his own head.

Denis is one of the patron saints of France and, perhaps inevitably, is invoked by those suffering from headache, which accounts for his inclusion among the Fourteen Holy Helpers.

St Denis. Cathedral of Sainte-Marie, Bayonne, France.

The Martyrdom of St Laurence. Polychrome wood relief, sixteenth century.
Salamanca Cathedral, Spain.

ST LAURENCE

Laurence, born perhaps in Spain around 230, was one of the earliest martyrs of the Church in Rome, where he served as almsgiver to Pope Sixtus II. At this period of persecution of Christians, after the execution of the pope himself, Laurence was commanded by the Emperor Valerian to surrender the Church's wealth to the state. Begging a three days' respite, Laurence distributed the wealth among the city's needy. When called to account by the emperor, he allegedly pointed to the city's poor and sick, saying: 'Behold the Church's treasure.' For this he was executed in 258, most likely by beheading.

According to his legend, Laurence's martyrdom was spectacularly cruel, for the story goes that he was roasted alive on a gridiron. At one point the stoical saint reputedly told his tormentors to turn him over because his first side was cooked through. Somewhat bizarrely, he is today the patron saint of cooks! In art he is represented together with his emblem the gridiron or grill.

In Rome, Laurence follows immediately behind Peter and Paul in importance. Besides his burial place in San Lorenzo fuori le Mura (St Laurence Outside the Walls), there are thirty Roman churches dedicated to him, as well as many thousands more worldwide.

Shooting stars were once traditionally called the 'fiery tears of St Laurence' because one of the periodic swarms of these meteors (the Perseids) occurs around his feast day of 10 August.

ST APOLLONIA

Apollonia was a third-century deaconess of Alexandria, Egypt, during a period of persecution of Christians in that part of the Roman world. In 249, when she was apparently already advanced in years, she became a victim of state-condoned mob violence. Her assailants smashed her teeth out and threatened her with burning unless she renounced her faith, whereupon she leapt of her own volition into the fire that had been prepared for her.

Apollonia's legend elaborates on this story. In it she has become a beautiful young woman who, for her faith, is tortured (sometimes by her own father) through having her teeth pulled out with pincers.

Theologically, this saint proved an interesting case for early churchmen, who debated whether or not her self-immolation qualified her as a genuine martyr. However, what has fascinated artists (including Andy Warhol, in four screenprints of 1984, themselves copied from a painting from the fifteenth-century workshop of Piero della Francesca) was the refined cruelty of her torture. She is represented as a young woman holding a tooth in a pair of pincers.

As might almost be expected, Apollonia is invoked against toothache and is the patron saint of dentists. Worldwide there are numerous dental societies, dentistry students' clubs, and so forth, named for her.

St Apollonia. Polychrome wood altar statue, *c.* 1628, by Philipp Dirr. Cathedral of St Maria and St Korbinian, Freising, Bavaria.

St Agatha. Fresco medallion, 1464, by Benozzo Gozzoli.
Church of Sant'Agostino, San Gimignano, Tuscany.

ST AGATHA

This saint was born in Sicily, perhaps in Catania or Palermo, about the year 225. While authenticated details about her life are few, other than that she was martyred under the Emperor Decius around 250, her legends are many. According to these, she was sought in marriage by a Roman magistrate, a pagan, whom she refused because she had dedicated herself as a virgin to Christ. Under Roman law, he then had her as a Christian arrested and subjected to various tortures, including burning and having her breasts cut off. St Peter was said to have appeared to her and healed her, but she eventually died in prison from her sufferings. When Mount Etna erupted in the year following her death, her veil was carried through the streets of Catania and the eruption ceased, a deliverance ascribed to the saint's intervention.

Agatha is a unique figure in art, as she is shown carrying her own breasts on a salver. She may also bear a pair of pincers, with which she was tortured. Since her breasts in some early depictions looked like bread rolls, loaves of 'St Agatha's bread' were, and still are, blessed in some places on her feast day of 5 February. She is invoked for protection from diseases of the breasts and from danger of fire and volcanic eruption. By a bizarre misunderstanding of a sort not uncommon in the iconography of saints, she is also the patron of bell-founders because her breasts in some representations may look like little inverted bells.

ST HELEN

Born in Bythinia, in today's Turkey, about the year 250, Helen was the daughter of an innkeeper and the mother of the future Roman Emperor Constantine. It was he who first granted religious freedom to Christians throughout the Empire in 313. Helen had been married to the general Constantius Chlorus (Constantine's father), but when he became emperor he divorced her in favour of a socially and politically more suitable wife. Helen did not convert to Christianity until she was in her sixties, but was then zealous in her observances, building churches and caring for the poor. She is supposed, on a visit to Palestine, to have excavated the cross on which Jesus died at Calvary. She also built basilicas on the Mount of Olives and at Bethlehem, and she died in the East around 330, though her personal relics now rest mostly in Rome. Whether the cross that Helen found was indeed the true cross or not, it assumed enormous importance, and pieces of it, or of wood that had reputedly touched it, as well as nails perhaps from it, were widely and often fraudulently peddled and disseminated as relics during the Middle Ages.

Helen is portrayed as a lady with her attribute of a large cross, or finding a large cross.

The island of Saint Helena in the South Atlantic was named for the saint, it having been discovered by the Portuguese in 1502 on St Helen's Day (21 May as celebrated in the Eastern Church). After his defeat at Waterloo, Napoleon Bonaparte was imprisoned there until his death in 1821.

St Helen. Statue on Baroque façade, 1741–4, of Church of Santa Croce in Gerusalemme, Rome, by Domenico Gregorini and Pietro Passalacqua.

ST ANTHONY THE GREAT

The Egyptian hermit Anthony is regarded as the founder of Christian monasticism (though Western monasticism stems from the work of Benedict in sixth-century Italy). He was born near Memphis, Egypt, around 250, and at an early age, after the death of his parents, withdrew from the world to live with a group of ascetics. Later, between about 286 and 306, he dwelt in complete isolation at an abandoned military fort at

Pispir. Others were drawn to him, and he founded the earliest monastic community, with himself as 'abbot', at Fayum, Egypt, about 306. Anthony lived to be over a hundred, dying around 356.

In pictorial art the saint is portrayed as an old and bearded hermit with a T-shaped staff, which is also an ancient form of the cross (Tau cross). Often he appears in the wilderness, tormented by devils or beset by temptations in the form of lascivious women. Or he may be shown visiting another desert hermit, on which occasion the two are brought a loaf of bread by a raven. This scene has been depicted by Dürer and by Velázquez in his famous painting *St Anthony Abbot and St Paul the Hermit*, in the Prado, Madrid.

During the Middle Ages an Order of Hospitallers of St Anthony ministered to the sick in western Europe. To attract almsgivers, the hospitallers would ring little bells. Pigs belonging to the order were licensed to roam and feed freely, and to them, too, bells were attached in order to show their ownership. Anthony is therefore sometimes depicted with a pig or a bell, his emblems, as in Piero di Cosimo's painting of *The Visitation with Saints Nicholas and Anthony* (see page 33).

Of etymological interest: a tantony (St Anthony) pig is the smallest pig of a litter. Tantony is also the name given to a small church bell, or to any hand bell.

Saint Anthony Tormented by Demons. Copper engraving, *c.*1470–75, by Martin Schongauer.

ST JUSTA & ST RUFINA

Martyred in Spain during the Diocletian persecutions of the third century, the sisters Justa and Rufina accompany each other in art as they did in life and in death. They were the daughters of a potter in Seville and earned a living by selling their father's wares, keeping only enough money to live on and giving the rest to charity. When asked to provide pottery for the worship of the Roman goddess Venus, they refused to do so, and instead shattered their pots and destroyed the statue of the goddess. They were consequently put to death, one version of their lives recounting that they were thrown to the lions.

The sisters are portrayed together holding palms of martyrdom, and are sometimes shown with pottery (perhaps broken) or a lion. They usually appear with the pointed Moorish tower, the Giralda, of Seville Cathedral in the background. Reputedly, the invocation of the two saints averted the destruction of the Giralda in a violent thunderstorm in 1504. For that reason they are the patronesses of Seville.

Saint Justa and Saint Rufina. Oil on canvas, 1665–6,
by Bartolomé Esteban Murillo. Museo de Bellas Artes, Seville.

ST PHILOMENA

The cult of Philomena was probably the shortest-lived on record: approved only in 1835, it was abolished again little more than a hundred years later. Though one continues to see prayer cards and statues to Philomena today, and books and internet websites still promote her cult, there never actually existed a saint of this name. It was supposed for a time that she had been a virgin martyred in Rome in ancient times for her Christian faith. She first attracted attention in 1802 when the bones of a young girl (allegedly identified by an inscription as 'Philomena') and a phial said to contain her blood were found in the Roman Catacomb of Priscilla. When the remains were removed to the church of Mugnano del Cardinale near Naples in 1805, miracles attributed to Philomena's intercession were reported, legends grew up around her name, and her cult became widespread. It was annulled again in 1961, and her shrine at Mugnano was deconsecrated, because nothing was known of the life or personality of the girl to justify sainthood.

Philomena is portrayed as a pretty young girl in long Roman robes and holding an anchor (a traditional Christian symbol of hope) and the arrow with which she was supposedly slain.

St Philomena. Polychrome wood statue, nineteenth century.
Parish Church of Our Lady (Upper Parish), Bamberg, Bavaria.

ST BLAISE

Little is known with certainty about the life of Blaise, who lived in Armenia in the third century though his main cult did not originate until about the eighth century. He is believed to have been a bishop and to have been martyred by the Romans.

Many legends attach to Blaise's name. The most notable relates how he miraculously retrieved a fish bone from the throat of a choking child. When the Roman authorities later imprisoned him, the child's mother brought food and candles to him in prison. One of the Fourteen Holy Helpers, Blaise is invoked today still as a protector against diseases of the throat, such as diphtheria, and crossed candles are used to bless the throat in his name (the Blessing of St Blaise). He is said to have been martyred by being torn apart with wool combs before being beheaded. A painting by Sano di Pietro in Siena's Pinacoteca Nazionale vividly depicts his martyrdom.

Blaise is usually portrayed as a bishop with an emblem or emblems reflecting his legends: crossed candles or a comb.

St Blaise. Plaster, 1767–8, by Johann Michael Feichtmayr.
Altar of Mercy, Basilica and Pilgrimage Church of Vierzehnheiligen,
Bavaria. St Barbara stands in the left background.

ST CECILIA

The life of Cecilia as we know it is based almost entirely on legends. These originated mostly in the sixth century, though they locate her in third-century Rome. According to her story, Cecilia was a Christian girl who dedicated her virginity to Christ, but was nevertheless given in marriage to a pagan

named Valerian. When she explained her vow to him, he was so moved that both he and his brother converted to Christianity and were eventually martyred for their faith. Cecilia, too, was martyred. She was first boiled in water, and when this failed to kill her, she was beheaded.

Cecilia is the patron saint of music. Her association with music actually developed quite late, however, stemming as it does from a later, sixteenth-century account of her life according to which 'she sang only to God in her heart on her wedding day'. She is portrayed in art with various musical instruments, especially the organ, which legend claims she invented.

Cecilia has inspired musical compositions by Handel, Purcell and others, as well as literary works including Dryden's 'Song for St Cecilia's Day', Pope's 'Ode for Music on Saint Cecilia's Day', and 'The Second Nun's Tale' in Chaucer's *Canterbury Tales*.

Orpheus cou'd lead the savage race;
And Trees unrooted left their place;
Sequacious of the Lyre:
But bright CECILIA rais'd the wonder high'r;
When to her ORGAN, vocal Breath was giv'n
An Angel heard, and straight appear'd
Mistaking Earth for Heaven.

from Dryden, 'A Song for St Cecilia's Day'

St Cecilia. Oil on canvas, 1514, by Raphael. Pinacoteca Nazionale, Bologna. Cecilia (centre) is seen here with (from left to right) Sts Paul, John the Apostle, Peter and Mary Magdalene.

ST CHRISTOPHER

Few saints are more familiar in our age of travel than
Christopher, patron saint of travellers. Alas, Christopher's life
is almost entirely legendary, and it is closely linked with his
name, which in Greek means 'Christ bearer'. All that is

known of the historical
saint is that he probably
lived and died in Asia
Minor sometime in the
third century. Legend has
it that he was a giant
who, pledging to serve
only the greatest of all
masters, was on the point
of dedicating himself to
Satan. When he saw Satan
recoil from the sign of
the cross, however, he
determined instead to
become a Christian and to
serve God. He settled on
the bank of a river across
which he ferried travel-
lers. One day he agreed
to carry a tiny child across
and, almost collapsing
under the weight, he was
told that he was carrying

Jesus, who bears the weight of the whole world. The child told him to plant his staff in the ground, and on the following day the staff bore flowers and figs as a sign of the truth he had been told.

Christopher is shown as a (sometimes hirsute) giant carrying the Christ Child on his shoulder, generally across a river, and supporting his own weight on a staff or a tree trunk. It was believed that anyone who saw a picture or statue of Christopher would not die that day. Hence his image was, and still is, often placed in a prominent place – for instance, on the outside wall of a church or other public building, or on the dashboard of a car. He is one of the Fourteen Holy Helpers.

Owing to the largely fictitious character of Christopher's life, his cult was demoted from universal to merely local status in the Roman calendar of saints in 1969. In view of his celebrity status, this provoked strong opposition in some quarters for a time, including protests led by popular film stars in Italy, as David Farmer reports.

St Christopher. Oil on wood, *c.*1470, by Dieric Bouts the Younger.
Alte Pinakothek, Munich.

ST VALENTINE

Valentine's feast day of 14 February is his best known particular. There were, in fact, probably two third-century Italian saints called Valentine, one of whom was certainly a bishop of Terni in Umbria. It appears that both were beheaded with a sword. Otherwise little is known about either, and they have become conflated as simply 'Valentine'.

The custom of associating Valentine with romance possibly harkens back to the Roman Lupercalia, a fertility festival that fell on 15 February. In medieval folklore, 14 February was also the day that birds traditionally paired up. Chaucer's poem 'The Parlement of Foulys' (*c.* 1382) centres on a conference of various birds to choose their mates on Valentine's Day:

> For this was on seynt Valentynys day,
> Whan every byrd comyth there to chese his make
> Of every kynde that men thynke may,
> And that so heuge a noyse gan they make,
> That erthe & eyr & tre & every lake
> So ful was, that onethe was there space
> For me to stonde, so ful was al the place.

Images of Valentine show him as a bishop with his emblem of a sword – *not* with hearts, roses or cupids.

The love association of Valentine's Day plays an important part in Walter Scott's novel *The Fair Maid of Perth* (1828), subtitled *Saint Valentine's Day*. The novel provided the basis for Bizet's opera *La Jolie Fille de Perth* (1867).

St Valentine. Polychrome wood statue, 1696, by Georg Pämer.
Church of Mariä Himmelfahrt, Grassau, Chiemgau, Bavaria.

ST NICHOLAS OF MYRA

Nicholas is the patron of children and has become known as Santa Claus throughout the English-speaking world. In some countries his feast day of 6 December is the traditional day for Christmas gift giving.

Little is verifiable about Nicholas's actual life, though it is thought that he was born in Patras, Greece, about the year 280. Certainly he became Bishop of Myra, in today's Turkey, at some point in the fourth century. During the Roman persecution of Christians he was imprisoned and tortured, but was eventually released and died in Myra about 345.

Three main legends are reflected in Nicholas's iconography. In the first of these, a father consigns his three daughters to a brothel so that they can earn enough money for a dowry with which to marry. To save them, Nicholas throws three gold balls (or bags or bars of gold) through their window. A second legend has him rescue three boys from being pickled in a tub of brine by a butcher. On the basis of these stories he became the patron saint of children. A further legend relates how he rescued sailors from a ship during a storm, for which reason he is also a patron of sailors. Perhaps because of his 'redemption' of the three girls, he also became the patron saint of pawn-brokers, some of whom still use his emblem of three gold balls to identify their shops.

After the fall of the city of Myra to the Moslems, Nicholas's relics were taken by sea to Bari in southern Italy in 1087. Since then his cult has spread far and wide. Most portrayals show him as a bishop, often holding three gold balls, as he

appears in a fresco in the Basilica of Santa Cristina, Bolsena (see page 135). Alternatively, he is shown with three boys in a tub, or with a ship, as in Gentile da Fabriano's dramatic portrayal of *St Nicholas Saving a Storm-tossed Ship* in the Vatican Pinacoteca. Images of Santa Claus bear little resemblance to the Nicholas of fact or legend.

St Nicholas. Panel of oak door, early sixteenth century, by Francisco de Colonia. Church of San Nicolás, Burgos, Spain.

ST ALBAN

Reputedly the earliest of England's martyrs, Alban is known as the English protomartyr. His life, however, is largely legendary. He was supposedly a prominent Romano-British citizen of Verulamium (today's St Albans in Hertfordshire), who sheltered a priest in his home during the Roman persecution of Christians at the end of the third or the beginning of the fourth century. Alban was so impressed by the priest's deportment that he converted to Christianity himself and was baptized. He also changed clothes with the priest, enabling the latter to escape but bringing about his own arrest. When he subsequently refused to sacrifice to the pagan gods, he was first flogged, and then condemned to death by beheading.

Alban, little seen outside of England, is recognizable as a young man in a Roman tunic or toga. He may sometimes appear as a Roman soldier and bear a palm of martyrdom and a sword, as in Charles Kempe's stained-glass window in the Lady Chapel of St Albans Cathedral.

Albanus. Mosaic, 2001, by Christopher Hobbs.
Westminster Cathedral, London.

ST PANCRAS

The name of St Pancras has a familiar ring in British ears, for it has been given to a district of London and to a major railway station. In both cases the name stems from the north London church of St Pancras. Though probably little more than that is generally known about him, the earliest church founded in England by St Augustine of Canterbury was actually dedicated to this saint.

As is so often the case, legend makes good what even history does not know. Here legend relates that Pancras was born around 290 in Phrygia, in Asia Minor, and that at the age of fourteen he fell victim to the Diocletian persecutions. Apparently he was early left an orphan and was brought by an uncle to Rome, where both were converted to Christianity. Pancras used his inheritance to relieve the travails of persecuted Christians before being himself martyred around 304. He was buried in a catacomb on the Via Aurelia, where a church was built on his grave around 500. Today's Basilica of San Pancrazio fuori le Mura later superseded this.

Pancras appears as a beardless young man in Roman dress. He carries a palm of martyrdom and a book, sometimes with the text: *'Venite ad me et ego dabo vobis omnia bona'* ('Come to me and I shall give you all things good'). These words, precisely quoted from the Latin Vulgate Bible (Genesis 48: 18), are those spoken by Joseph to his starving and destitute brothers in Egypt. They may, then, be said to hold out a promise of assistance from Pancras to those in dire need.

Together with Servatius and Boniface, Pancras is one of the

so-called Ice Saints. Their feast days of 12 to 14 May are notorious for the last frosts of the year:

Till Pancras, Servatius and Boniface are past
Cold winter hasn't breathed his last.

Farmers' Almanac

St Pancras. Polychrome wood statue.
Church of San Sebastián, Madrid.

ST URSULA

Ursula's life story is based almost entirely on legend. Supposedly she was the daughter of a third- or fourth-century Christian British king, who betrothed her to a pagan prince. Because she really wished to remain a virgin, however, she was allowed to postpone the marriage for three years. During this time she sailed to Europe with eleven attendants and went on a pilgrimage as far as Rome. On their return, by way of the River Rhine, pagan Huns in Cologne took them captive, and Ursula's companions were raped and murdered. When she herself refused to marry the heathen king, she was killed with an arrow. She was subsequently buried with her attendants in Cologne, whose church of St Ursula claims to possess her relics today. The number of her companions escalated from eleven to eleven thousand through an error in accounts of her life during the tenth century. (The abbreviation XIMV, meaning 'eleven martyred virgins', was evidently read as 'eleven thousand virgins'!)

Ursula was much venerated in the Middle Ages. Because so little is known about her, however, her cult was demoted from universal to local in the 1969 reform of the Roman calendar.

In artistic portrayals Ursula is usually shown wearing her princess's crown and holding the arrow or arrows with which she was martyred. She may also be shown sheltering her maidens, or children, under her cloak. The city of Cologne, whose patron she is, commemorates her story through eleven black ermine tails in its municipal coat of arms.

St Ursula Shrine: St Ursula and the Holy Virgins. On wood, 1489, by Hans Memling. Memlingmuseum, Sint-Janshospitaal, Bruges, Belgium.

St Expeditus. Printed prayer card from Italy.

ST EXPEDITUS

There is no proof that Expeditus ever actually existed, though the *Roman Martyrology* lists him as one of a number of saints martyred in Melitine, Armenia (no year given). His cult no doubt arose through a pun on his name, which suggests that he should be invoked in cases of urgency, in order to 'expedite' matters. Delaney writes that 'popular devotion to him may have mistakenly developed when a crate of holy relics from the Catacombs in Rome to a convent in Paris was mistakenly identified by the recipients as St Expeditus by the word *expedito* [dispatched] written on the crate.' There is probably no truth to this amusing story either, however.

In any event, the cult of Expeditus is still alive and well today. The authors of this book have in their possession prayer cards to Expeditus in English and Spanish, printed in Italy and purchased in the United States, and another in Portuguese from Brazil. All of these cards show him, characteristically, as a Roman soldier holding a palm of martyrdom and a cross, with the words *'Hodie'* (Latin: today) and *'Cras'* (Latin: tomorrow), implying that a prayer to him might help expedite a difficult matter from one day to the next. The Brazilian picture and its captions are printed in reverse, however, perhaps inadvertently suggesting that expeditiousness may not always produce the very best results.

ST GEORGE

George would at first seem one of those saints whose very existence might be called in question. How real, after all, can a man have been whose life is inextricably intertwined with a dragon (unless, of course, one believes in dragons)? To get at the real George, then, one must sift probable fact from fiction. It appears most likely that in early-fourth-century Palestine a certain George was martyred for his faith. He was probably a soldier, and was executed for refusing to sacrifice to the pagan gods. This George was venerated long before the rise of his legends, which date from the Middle Ages.

According to legend, George was a soldier who freed a princess from a dragon to which animals and, later, humans were sacrificed in order to prevent it from ravaging the land. Here we have the essentials of George's story as it is familiar in art: the knight, sometimes on horseback, subduing a dragon with spear or sword while occasionally a maiden looks on. This legend can be interpreted symbolically as the believer (the Christian soldier) defending the Church (the maiden) against Satan (the dragon). Symbolic value notwithstanding, the cult of George (whose feast day is 23 April) has since 1969 been reduced in the Catholic Church from universal to local.

Because of his defence of the maiden and the Palestinian setting of his legend, George became popular in Europe during the chivalric period of the crusades. He is the patron saint of soldiers, of Boy Scouts and of England, among other countries.

G. K. Chesterton has portrayed him in a humorous light:

St George he was for England,
And before he killed the dragon
He drank a pint of English ale
Out of an English flagon.

St George he was for England,
And right gallantly set free
The lady left for dragon's meat
And tied up to a tree . . .
from 'The Englishman'

St George. Polychrome
stone relief,
*c.*1924. Soldiers' Chapel,
Lincoln Cathedral.

ST COSMAS & ST DAMIAN

Cosmas and Damian were twin bothers, inseparable in life and in death. Though nothing is known with certainty about their lives, there is some evidence that martyrs bearing these names were put to death in Cyrrhus, Syria, during the persecutions of the Emperor Diocletian around the beginning of the fourth century. Legend relates that they were both physicians. Much loved for their Christian charity, they were called the 'holy moneyless ones' and cared for the indigent sick without charging fees.

The saintly twins appear as similar, usually young, men in red doctors' robes with instruments of their profession, such as mortar and pestle, or with ointment, medicinal herbs or a box of pills. They may sometimes be pictured performing an operation. Along with Luke, they are the patron saints of physicians.

The Healing of Justinian by St Cosmas and St Damian. Tempera on wood, 1438–40, by Fra Angelico. Museo di San Marco, Florence. In this spectacular operation, the saints graft the leg of a black man on to the body of a white man whose own leg has had to be amputated!

ST MARGARET OF ANTIOCH

Though legends about Margaret abound, she probably never existed. Her cult became popular in Europe during the crusades, but was deleted from the Roman calendar in 1969.

According to legend, Margaret was the daughter of a pagan priest of Antioch, in today's Turkey. On converting to Christianity, she was repudiated by her father and became a shepherdess. Refusing marriage to the governor of Antioch, she was denounced by him as a Christian and was subjected under Roman law to various spectacular tortures. One story tells how, when in prison, she was swallowed alive by a dragon, which then burst asunder and released her. She is supposed to have effected mass conversions of people who, like her, were then martyred under the Emperor Diocletian at the beginning of the fourth century.

Perhaps because of how she emerged unscathed from the dragon, women in childbirth traditionally invoked Margaret. As such she is one of the Fourteen Holy Helpers and was in the past one of the most venerated saints in Europe. Margaret is pictured with, or trampling on or slaying, a dragon.

The Marriage of St Catherine. Tempera on wood, *c.*1500, by an unknown Hungarian master. Hungarian National Gallery, Budapest. St Margaret of Antioch is shown on the right of this picture. The others, from left to right, are Barbara, Catherine of Alexandria, the Virgin and Dorothy. The four female saints, without the Virgin, are known as the Virgines Capitales.

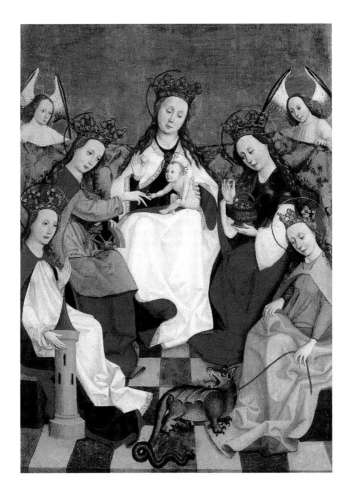

ST SEBASTIAN

Little is known about the historical Sebastian, who was martyred under the Emperor Diocletian around the year 300 and was buried in a cemetery on the Appian Way, south of Rome, near the church that today bears his name. According to legend he was a Christian who assisted persecuted Christians though he was himself a soldier and a member of the Roman Imperial Guard. In his turn he, too, was persecuted and ultimately martyred for his faith. He was ordered to be shot to death with arrows, but survived this and was subsequently clubbed to death.

Sebastian is portrayed as a young man (sometimes a soldier), generally partly nude and tied to a tree, a post or a column, and pierced with arrows. This combination of sexuality and cruelty has made him one of the most frequently depicted saints – for example, by Botticelli, Bellini and El Greco.

Like George, Sebastian is a patron of soldiers, but ironically also of archers and arrowsmiths. Since the arrows appear to stick in his body like pins in a cushion, he became additionally the patron saint of pinmakers! During the Middle Ages, Sebastian (like Roch) was invoked against the plague, which was said to strike as swiftly as an arrow. For that reason he is included among the Fourteen Holy Helpers.

St Sebastian. Wood processional staff, 1790.
Church of St Andreas, Elbach, Bavaria.

ST CRISPIN &
ST CRISPINIAN

The historical Crispin and Crispinian were probably Romans martyred for their Christian faith around the year 300. Because their relics were translated from Rome to Soissons, France, in the sixth century, however, most of their legends are set in that area. Tradition claims that they were Roman brothers and shoemakers who went as missionaries to Gaul. Here they preached during the day, while at night they supported themselves by making and repairing shoes instead of living on alms. Angels supplied them with the necessary leather. In depictions the brothers figure as shoemakers with shoes or the tools of their trade, such as knife, last, hammer or awl. As might be expected, they are the patron saints of shoemakers, cobblers and leather-workers.

The Battle of Agincourt (1415), in which the English won a great victory over the French in the Hundred Years' War, was fought on the feast day of Crispin and Crispinian (25 October). Hence Shakespeare's Henry V, in his address to his troops on the eve of battle, asserts:

And Crispin Crispian shall ne'er go by
From this day to the ending of the world
But we in it shall be remembered.

Henry V, iv, iii

St Crispin and St Crispinian. Polychrome wood altar, sixteenth century.
Church of San Vicente, Ávila, Spain.

ST BARBARA

Barbara is one of those saints whose stories fascinate but who probably never existed, though she was supposedly executed during the Roman persecution of Christians about 303. Her legendary life was not written until the seventh century. According to her story, Barbara was a beautiful maiden who was confined in a tower by her heathen father to safeguard her from the attentions of men. During one of his absences, she became a Christian and withdrew as a hermit to a little two-windowed bath-house, to which she added a third window in honour of the trinity. Enraged at her conversion, her father handed her over for punishment to a Roman magistrate, who, after a number of unsuccessful attempts to kill her, ordered her father to cut off her head with a sword. The father himself was then struck dead by a bolt of lightning.

Barbara is most commonly represented with her tower, usually three-windowed. Alternatively, she may be shown with a chalice and host, representing her turning to Christianity, as in a celebrated painting by Hans Holbein the Elder in the Alte Pinakothek, Munich. Because of her association with the death by lightning of her father, she became the patron saint of those in danger of sudden death by lightning, fire or explosion – notably of artillerists and miners. This merited her inclusion among the Fourteen Holy Helpers.

Branches from a fruit tree or flowering shrub cut on St Barbara's Day (4 December) and kept in water in a warm room will flower by Christmas. This is known as a 'St Barbara's bouquet' in Germany. Though Barbara, as fictitious, was

struck from the Roman calendar of saints in 1969, one can still make such a bouquet successfully today.

St Barbara. Fresco, 1471, by Domenico Ghirlandaio.
Church of Sant'Andrea, Cecina, Tuscany.

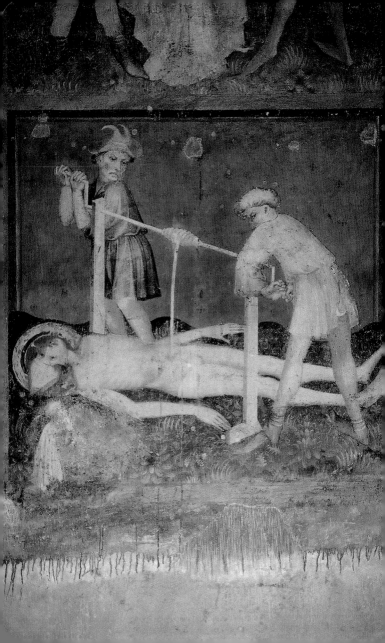

ST ELMO

Elmo (Latin: Erasmus) exemplifies how confused and confusing the stories of some saints can be. Little is known about the real Elmo other than that he was a bishop of Formiae, Italy, who was martyred around 303. His legend makes him a Syrian bishop who was subjected to various tortures during the persecutions of Diocletian. He was beaten, rolled in pitch and set on fire, and then thrown into prison, from which an angel released him. Another angel transported him to the temporary refuge of Formiae. His legend also has him preaching during a thunderstorm, quite unperturbed by a thunderbolt striking nearby – which explains his later patronage of sailors, who had ample reason to fear thunderstorms. 'St Elmo's fire' is the name given to the mysterious light that sometimes plays around the masts of ships during or after a storm.

Because of his patronage of sailors, Elmo's emblem is a capstan or windlass. Due to a misunderstanding, however, it was thought at one point that he was martyred by having his intestines pulled out by a windlass, as can be seen in some depictions of him. Because of this link with intestines, he was invoked by all of those, especially children, who suffer from problems of the digestive tract. Little wonder that Elmo figures among the Fourteen Holy Helpers!

The Martyrdom of St Elmo. On a stone pillar, *c.* 1450, attributed to Erasmus Schüchlin. Ulm Cathedral, Germany.

ST LUCY

Little is known about the historical Lucy (Latin: Lucia) other than that she died in Syracuse, Sicily, about 304 during Diocletian's persecutions and that she was early venerated as a virgin martyr. Her various legends are highly dramatic, but historically worthless. According to these, she was a beautiful and wealthy Sicilian girl who refused all marriage offers because she had dedicated herself to Christ. For this, Roman law condemned her to numerous cruel punishments (including being committed to a brothel and being burned at the stake), but she survived all of these unscathed. She also had her eyes put out, but they were miraculously restored to her. Finally, she was slain with a sword.

Lucy is shown as a young woman bearing her own eyes on a plate. Those suffering from eye problems invoke her.

St Lucy's Day, 13 December, being near the shortest day of the year, is celebrated in Sweden as a festival of light in anticipation of the days growing longer. The saint's eyes and her name (derived from Latin *lux*) are both suggestive of light.

St Lucy. On wood. Church of Santa Maria del Popolo, Rome.

ST FLORIAN

Florian was born in the latter half of the third century in Zeiselmauer near Vienna, Austria, which at that time formed part of the Roman Empire. Though baptized and brought up a Christian, he served for some years as an officer in the Roman army. For refusing under the Emperor Diocletian to abjure Christianity and sacrifice to the pagan gods, he was first tortured and then drowned in the River Enns near Lorch in about the year 304.

Because of his association with water, Florian is invoked for protection against flood, but above all against fire (he is the patron saint of firefighters). He is usually represented as a Roman soldier pouring water from a bucket to extinguish a burning building. He is much venerated in Austria and Bavaria, especially in rural areas, where fires caused by accident or lightning strikes can be particularly devastating. One quite often sees pictures of him painted on the outside walls of farmhouses.

There is a popular German prayer to St Florian, one hopes not meant entirely seriously:

Heiliger Sankt Florian, du Wasserkübelmann,
Verschon' mein Haus, zünd' andere an.
(Holy St Florian, with your bucket of water,
Spare my house, set fire to other people's.)

St Florian. Plaster devotional statuette, *c.*1975.
Private collection.

ST CHRISTINA OF BOLSENA

An early Italian virgin martyr, Christina was put to death for refusing to sacrifice to the Roman gods, perhaps around 304, under Diocletian. Legend claims that she survived burning and an attempt to drown her by throwing her into Lake Bolsena with a millstone around her neck. She was finally shot to death with arrows. Her shrine can be visited today in Bolsena, Tuscany.

Christina is generally portrayed as a young woman with a millstone, her emblem.

St Christina with St Nicholas of Myra. Detail of fresco, fifteenth century, of the Sienese School. Basilica of Santa Cristina, Bolsena, Tuscany.

ST AGNES

Agnes was an early Roman martyr who died around 305 and about whose life little is known with certainty. Legend relates that, while still a girl, she refused to marry because she had dedicated her virginity to Christ. Imperial edicts against Christianity were then invoked against her. After many humiliations and tortures, including being consigned to a brothel and being half burned at the stake, she was killed by having her throat pieced with a sword.

Agnes is recognizable in art by the lamb that she holds or which accompanies her. The lamb is not linked with her life story, but puns on her name (Latin *agnus* meaning lamb). Unlike St Geneviève, whose emblem is also a lamb or a sheep, Agnes, as a martyr, may additionally bear a palm branch, signifying victory over death.

An ancient tradition says that if certain practices are followed on St Agnes's Eve (the eve of 21 January) a person will dream of his or her future wife or husband. Keats treats this theme in his poem 'The Eve of St Agnes', where one reads how on that day,

Young virgins might have visions of delight,
And soft adorings from their loves receive
Upon the honey'd middle of the night,
If ceremonies due they did aright . . .

Tennyson's poem 'St Agnes' Eve' develops its subject in religious terms, for in it Jesus is the heavenly bridegroom of whom a cloistered nun dreams.

St Agnes. Oil on canvas, c. 1620, by Domenichino.
Royal Collection, Windsor.

ST DOROTHY

Dorothy was supposedly a virgin martyr who met her end at Caesarea, Asia Minor, during the persecutions of Diocletian in the early fourth century. Legend relates that when on her way to her execution she was mocked by a young lawyer, Theophilus, who told her to send him fruits from the garden of Paradise where she was going. After her death, an angel appeared and presented Theophilus with a basket containing three apples and three roses. Theophilus himself then converted and was later martyred. Since her life is apocryphal, Dorothy's cult was suppressed in 1969.

The patron saint of florists, Dorothy is depicted with a basket, or apron, containing fruit and flowers, sometimes also with a crown of flowers on her head. Her story forms the basis of the tragedy *The Virgin Martir* (1621) by Massinger and Dekker and of poems by Swinburne ('St Dorothy') and Gerard Manley Hopkins. Hopkins's poem, in which the poet speaks with the voice of Dorothy herself, does not describe any known picture of the saint:

I bear a basket lined with grass.
I am so light and fair
Men are amazed to watch me pass
With the basket that I bear,
Which in newly drawn green litter
Carries treats of sweet for bitter.
See my lilies; lilies none,
None in Caesar's garden blow.

Quinces, look, when not one
Is set in any orchard; no,
Not set because their buds not spring;
Spring not for world is wintering.

From G.M. Hopkins, 'Lines for a picture of St Dorothy'

Madonna and Child with Mary Magdalene and St Dorothea. On wood, *c.* 1325,
by Ambrogio Lorenzetti. Pinacoteca Nazionale, Siena.

ST VITUS

There apparently lived a real boy named Vitus who was put to death under the Roman Emperor Diocletian in the early years of the fourth century. Around this figure numerous legends accumulated. Vitus was supposedly a boy convert who fled his native Sicily to the Italian mainland to avoid persecution. In Rome he miraculously cured Diocletian's son of epilepsy, but this did not prevent the cruel despot from imprisoning him and subjecting him to various tortures (including being boiled in oil together with a rooster), from which, however, he emerged unscathed. Vitus was freed from his prison when a thunderstorm fortuitously destroyed a number of pagan temples, after which an angel conducted him back to Sicily. In the end, however, he is said to have been martyred either in Rome or in Sicily at the age of only seven (or twelve).

This saint is depicted as a young boy either in or bearing the pot or cauldron in which he was boiled. He may also be shown with a rooster.

One of the Fourteen Holy Helpers, Vitus was invoked against numerous major and minor calamities, including epilepsy, rabies, snakebite, thunderstorms and bed-wetting. Because of his association with epilepsy, the affliction known as St Vitus's dance (Sydenham's chorea) was named for him. This link with 'dancing' accounts somewhat curiously for his patronage of dancers and actors, while he is the patron, too, of young people and of many cities, including Prague, whose cathedral dedicated to him possesses some of his supposed relics.

St Vitus. Processional staff with wood figure and metal pot, eighteenth century. Church of St Martin, Amberg, Bavaria.

ST CATHERINE
OF ALEXANDRIA

Though Catherine was supposed to have lived in the fourth century, there is no mention of her until the beginning of a cult in the ninth century. Hence she is considered spurious

today, and her cult was deleted from the Roman calendar of saints in 1969. According to her legends, Catherine was a beautiful patrician maiden of Alexandria, Egypt. After having converted to Christianity, she rebuked the Roman emperor for his paganism and defeated in argument fifty philosophers appointed by him to convince her of her error. These philosophers themselves, indeed, converted to Christianity! Refusing to marry the emperor, who resolved to vanquish her through matrimony if by no other means, she was condemned to death by being bound to a spiked wheel. The wheel flew apart, however (injuring some onlookers), whereupon she was beheaded with a sword.

The spectacular character of Catherine's story, as well as her imputed wisdom and intellect, contributed much to her popularity. She is the patron saint of young girls, students, the clergy, philosophers, and those, like wheelwrights, spinners and millers, who work with wheels. She is included among the Fourteen Holy Helpers, and in pictures and statues is easily recognizable by her wheel (sometimes shattered), while she may also carry a sword as the instrument of her martyrdom. The firework known as the Catherine wheel was named after her.

St Catherine of Alexandria. Oil on canvas, *c.* 1598, by Caravaggio. Thyssen-Bornemisza Collection, Madrid.

ST MARTIN

Martin is credited with being the earliest post-biblical saint who was not also a martyr. The son of a pagan officer in the Roman army, he was born in Pannonia (today's Hungary) around 316. He himself became a soldier at an early age, and when on a tour of duty in Gaul had an experience in Amiens that transformed his life. Accosted in the freezing cold by a near-naked beggar, he cut his cloak in half to share with him. That night he supposedly had a dream in which it was revealed that the beggar had been Jesus. This resulted in his conversion to Christianity. Characteristically, Martin is portrayed as a mounted Roman soldier cutting his cloak with his sword.

The historical Martin played a vital part in the development of the Church in Gaul. At Ligugé, near Poitiers, he established about 361 a hermitage that soon became a centre for other worshippers and subsequently the earliest monastic community in the whole of France. From here he made missionary forays into adjacent parts of the country. Known for his piety and reputed as a miracle-worker, he was acclaimed bishop of the nearby city of Tours around 371. He remained bishop until his death in 397, and his relics rest in St Martin's Basilica in Tours.

In various parts of Europe there are children's lantern-light processions on St Martin's Day, 11 November. Because this day coincides with the migration of geese, goose was traditionally eaten on St Martin's Day, and he is occasionally shown in art with a goose, as in an altar statue in St Martin's Church in Amberg, Germany.

Cappella is the Late Latin term for the sort of cloak Martin wore and shared with the beggar. The English word 'chapel', like its cognates in other European languages, derives from the little shrine in which the Merovingian kings of France preserved the remains of the saint's *cappella*.

St Martin of Tours. Austrian folk art picture (*verre églomisé*), 1976.
Private collection.

ST JEROME

Jerome (Latin: Hieronymus) is one of the most important figures in Church history and, as a renowned scholar, is, together with Ambrose, Augustine and Gregory, one of the Latin Doctors of the Church. He was born in Stridon, Dalmatia (in present day Croatia), around 341. After baptism as a young man, he travelled in Gaul, Dalmatia and Italy, then spent five years as a hermit in the Syrian desert. Returning to Rome for

a time, he became secretary to Pope Damasus, but returned to the Holy Land, where he spent the last thirty-five years of his life. He built and lived in a small monastery in Bethlehem, where he also died in 420, though he is entombed in the Basilica of Santa Maria Maggiore, Rome.

Jerome's outstanding achievement as a scholar was his translation, in part a re-translation, into Latin of the original Hebrew and Greek scriptures (completed around 404). Known as the Vulgate, this Bible became the standard Latin version for the Catholic Church from the Council of Trent (1545–63) until 1979.

Perhaps because of his irascible disposition, Jerome, who was constantly in conflict with other churchmen, was never actually canonized. He is, therefore, unusual (though not unique), as a historically authenticated, yet paradoxically 'uncanonized' saint.

Jerome is usually depicted as an aged, bearded man sitting at a desk in front of his bible. Because he served as the pope's secretary, he sometimes wears, or has with him, a cardinal's wide-brimmed red hat, though he never actually became a cardinal (an office not yet established in his day). Sometimes a lion lies at his feet because of a legend that he removed a thorn from a lion's paw. Typical, too, are representations of him as a bearded hermit with a skull (in Caravaggio's *St Jerome*, in the Galleria Borghese, Rome), or striking his breast with a stone (in engravings by Dürer and Baldung Grien).

St Jerome in His Study. Wood engraving, 1492, by Albrecht Dürer.

ST AMBROSE

Ambrose was born in the Roman city of Trier, in today's Germany, about 339 and died in Milan in 397. Well educated in Italy, he rose to become a Roman provincial governor with his seat in Milan. Here in 374 he participated in an official capacity in the election of a new bishop. During the proceedings, so the story goes, a child's voice cried 'Ambrose for bishop!' At the time Ambrose was not a priest nor even baptized. Within a week he was baptized, ordained and consecrated Bishop of Milan.

As one of the Church's foremost early theologians, this saint is one of the four Latin Doctors of the Church, together with Jerome, Gregory and Augustine (he is said to have brought Augustine to Christianity). He also wrote hymns, systematized church music (the Ambrosian Chant is named for him) and exercised a powerful influence on the cultural and political life of his age. Of interest in the context of this book, he encouraged veneration of the saints and their relics. Indeed, some people have criticized him for his excessive zeal and superstition in this.

Ambrose is generally portrayed as a bishop with a beehive, or with bees or a beekeeper's hat. A legend relates that a swarm of bees settled on his mouth when he was a child in his cradle. The reference to bees is attributable to his eloquence, or 'honeyed words', as a speaker, but also to his tireless work as a churchman. Other emblems include a scourge, symbolizing his opposition to heresy, as in Ambrogio Giovanni Figino's painting of *St Ambrose on Horseback Expelling the Arians* in the Castello Sforzesco, Milan. And, like other scholarly saints, he may carry a book (his writings) or be shown working at a desk.

A martyrs' basilica built by Ambrose himself in Milan was dedicated to him (Sant'Ambrogio) on his entombment there in 835. A mosaic in the church depicting him and dating from around 470 is perhaps the oldest portrayal of any Church father and is believed by some historians to be the oldest surviving depiction of any saint.

St Ambrose. Polychrome wood statue, early seventeenth century, on pulpit of Parish Church of Our Lady (Upper Parish), Bamberg, Bavaria.

ST AUGUSTINE

One of the foremost figures of the early Christian Church, Augustine was also an eminent theologian and a prolific author, and as such is one of the four Latin Doctors of the Church. Much is known about his life from his *Confessions*, which has been called the earliest autobiography in Western literature. Born in Tagaste, in today's Algeria, in 354, he received a Christian upbringing from his mother Monica (who is also a saint), but was not baptized until an adult. After studying rhetoric and philosophy, he became a lawyer, later a scholar and a teacher, in Rome and Milan. He also lived for fifteen years with a mistress, by whom he had a much-loved son. After prolonged internal conflict, however, he was converted through the influence of St Ambrose. Returning from Italy to Africa in 388, he was ordained a priest in 391. He became Bishop of Hippo in 396 and died in 430.

To an outstanding degree Augustine possessed learning, intellect, passion, spirituality and force of personality, all of which are reflected in writings through which he influenced Western thought perhaps more than any Christian since St Paul. Apart from his *Confessions*, he is known above all for his sermons and for longer works such as *On The Trinity* and *The City of God*. His theology has, however, not always been viewed positively – particularly through his gloomy emphasis on original sin, on the sinfulness of human sexuality and on predestination (in which he has been seen as a forerunner of John Calvin no less).

Augustine's stern personality was not of the sort to inspire picturesque legends. He is characteristically shown as a bishop

holding a book or writing at his desk, often together with one or more of the other Latin Doctors of the Church (Sts Jerome, Ambrose or Gregory). Or he may be depicted with St Monica, an elderly nun in a black habit. In statuary, he sometimes holds, or has on his breast, a heart flaming or pierced with arrows.

St Augustine. Fresco, 1480, by Sandro Botticelli.
Church of Ognissanti, Florence.

ST NINIAN

As is so often the case with early saints, little is known about the life of the historical Ninian; and scholarly interest in him today is calling much of that little into question. It would appear, however, that he was born in south-west Scotland in the latter part of the fourth century and as a young man may have spent some years studying in Rome. From here he reputedly returned to evangelize his native district of Galloway and the neighboring area. *En route* through France he may have visited Martin of Tours, to whom a church was dedicated in what is today the Scottish town of Whithorn. Certainly Ninian built a church there (the first stone church in Britain), which, being painted white, caused the surrounding settlement to be known as Candida Casa (White House). Through Old English *hwit aern* (white house) this gave rise to the modern place name of Whithorn. Ninian died as Bishop of Whithorn, probably around 432. It is worth noting that, if this date is correct, his work predated by more than a century that of the more celebrated Columba (*c.* 521–97), who christianized the more northern parts of Scotland.

Ninian is shown as a bishop with a chain or fetters as his emblem. This derives from a posthumous later medieval tradition, according to which he was, like St Leonard, credited with miraculously helping prisoners of war to escape from captivity.

Many churches and schools are dedicated to Ninian in Scotland, while in England he is perhaps more familiarly

known as Trinian. The comic film *The Belles of St Trinians* (1954, with Alastair Sim) is set in an English school for girls.

St Ninian. Outdoor mural, painted in 1997 by Amanda Sutherland, in Whithorn, Scotland. The mural, unfortunately, no longer exists.

ST. PATRICK

ST PATRICK

Veneration of Patrick has been carried far and wide by emigrants from Ireland, whose patron he is. New York City's Catholic cathedral is dedicated to him, while St Patrick's Day parades (on 17 March) have become a familiar phenomenon worldwide. Yet Patrick, born around 389, was not himself a native of Ireland, but most likely of some western part of Roman Britain – of Wales, England or Scotland.

The son of a Romano-British magistrate, when about sixteen Patrick was abducted from his homeland by raiders and sold into slavery in pagan Ireland. Here he lived for six years before escaping. After various adventures, he returned home, but left again for Gaul for a time. Either in Gaul or in Britain he studied for the priesthood, was consecrated a bishop and, in accordance with his own wishes, was sent to Ireland around 432. Here he set up his see in Armagh, where he built a cathedral and from where he made many missionary journeys, largely christianizing the island. He died around 461.

Patrick is said to have explained the trinity though analogy with the shamrock, which is now the Irish national emblem. Various legends tell how he drove the serpents out of Ireland. He is portrayed as a bishop trampling on a snake or snakes (symbolic, of course, of Satan) and commonly holding a shamrock.

St Patrick. Printed prayer card from Italy.

ST GENEVIÈVE

Geneviève was born at Nanterre, near Paris, around 422. The story that she was a shepherdess for a time as a girl is charming, but has no basis in fact. She early felt herself called to God, and on the death of her parents moved to Paris and took the veil of a dedicated virgin at the age of fifteen. At this time the region was under attack from the Frankish tribes under their leaders Childeric and Clovis. Geneviève interceded with them on behalf of the Parisians, and she also risked her own life to bring food into the besieged city. For deliverance from their enemies she called on the townspeople to fast and pray and to repent their own sins, a plea that was no more popular in her day than it would be in ours and which resulted in an attempt on her life. However, her leading of public prayers and fasting was believed to have caused the Huns under Attila to bypass Paris in 451, and she was regarded as the saviour of the city, whose patron she now is. She is credited with having averted other, later calamities, too, including an epidemic in 1129, when her relics were carried around the city. She died in 500.

Geneviève is generally portrayed with sheep or a lamb in reference to her legendary time as a shepherdess. She may carry the keys of the city of Paris in her girdle.

The Panthéon in Paris, a burial place of French national heroes, was the church of St Geneviève until it was secularized during the Revolution. It contains a famous series of frescoes by Puvis de Chavannes illustrating scenes from the saint's life.

St Geneviève. Church of St Jacques, Bergerac, France.

St Brigid. Stained-glass window, *c.*1901.
St Eunan's Cathedral, Letterkenny, County Donegal.

ST BRIGID

Brigid was born of humble parents near Kildare, Ireland, about 450. She is said to have been baptized by St Patrick himself and to have personally founded the important Kildare monastery, of which she was abbess. From this institution, which housed both men and women, though separately, she helped spread Christianity throughout the island. Until her death around 525, she reputedly exercised great authority not only over her own abbey, but also within the wider Celtic Church.

Few details are known about Brigid's real life, which appears to have been characterized above all by charity and compassion. Her legends, on the other hand, are numerous. These often link her with the multiplication of food – for example, of butter for the poor. Analogously, she is supposed to have changed bath water into beer, while her cows gave milk three times in one day to enable her to refresh some visiting bishops. Another legend relates that when she was called to the bed of a dying pagan chieftain she illustrated the story of the crucifixion for him by plaiting a cross out of rushes or straw from the floor. Such St Brigid's crosses are still made in Ireland today.

Brigid is usually represented as an abbess with a cow, emblematic of her humble origins. She is a patroness of Ireland.

ST BENEDICT

Benedict is known as the father of Western monasticism, for it was he who first formulated and codified the rules for monastic life in western Europe. He was born in the Italian town of Norcia, Umbria, around 480. Though never ordained a priest, he was early attracted to a life of prayer and of withdrawal from the world, and he drew like-minded men to him. An early monastic community formed around him at Subiaco in the Apennines. Then about 530 he founded the now famous monastery of Monte Cassino, between Naples and Rome, and about the same time completed his *Regula monachorum* (*Rule for Monks*), which prescribed poverty, chastity, obedience, prayer, study and various sorts of manual labour for monks. *'Orare est laborare, laborare est orare'* ('To pray is to work, to work is to pray') is a motto of the order called after him the Benedictines, though the words do not actually appear in his *Rule*. Benedict's strictness was not always appreciated, and at an early point some hermits tried unsuccessfully to poison him. He died a natural death at his abbey of Monte Cassino about 550.

The saint is represented as a long-bearded abbot or monk in black (the colour of the Benedictine habit) with a broken cup (of poison) or a raven carrying off a piece of (poisoned) bread in its beak. Sometimes he holds a book (his *Rule*) or a rod, symbolic of monastic discipline. He may occasionally be portrayed together with his (probably twin) sister Scholastica.

A celebrated product of Benedictine industry was Benedictine liqueur, made today still in Fécamp, Normandy, where it was originally produced by the monks in the local abbey.

St Benedict. Fresco on stone pillar, late fifteenth century.
Church of Sant'Agostino, San Gimignano, Tuscany.

ST SCHOLASTICA

Born in Norcia, Italy, around 480, Scholastica was the sister, perhaps the twin sister, of St Benedict. She is regarded as the first Benedictine nun, for it was under her brother's direction that she founded and became abbess of a convent at Plombariola, near his own abbey of Monte Cassino. On her death in 543, Benedict is said to have experienced a vision of her soul rising to heaven in the form of a dove. He buried her in the grave intended for himself, where he, too, was later interred.

Scholastica is typically shown as a Benedictine nun in a black habit, sometimes with her emblem of a dove. In art she is quite frequently seen in Benedict's company, while statues to each sometimes stand on either side of a church altar.

St Scholastica. Polychrome wood statue, eighteenth century.
Church of St Laurentius, Rottach-Egern, Bavaria.

ST BRENDAN

Brendan was an Irish abbot, born probably near Tralee about 485. He founded a considerable number of monasteries (for instance, at Clonfert, Annadown, Innishadroum and Ardfert) and also undertook missionary journeys through Ireland as well as to Scotland and England before his death around 575. Today, however, his fame rests less on his actual achievements than on his legendary travels. Notably the mediaeval romance *The Navigation of St Brendan* recounts his long voyage with some other monks from Ireland to the Land of Promise, an island in the Atlantic. Some people claim that his Land of Promise was the Canary Islands. Others assert that it was, rather, North America, and that Brendan was, therefore, the earliest European visitor to the New World! To demonstrate that this might at the very least have been possible, Tim Severin retraced Brendan's supposed voyage from Ireland to Newfoundland with some companions in 1976–7, recording their experiences in his book *The Brendan Voyage* (1978). Matthew Arnold wrote a ballad 'Saint Brendan' (1860), while the saint's epic exploits, real or imaginary, have inspired the splendid musical suite *The Brendan Voyage* (1980) by the English composer Shaun Davey. An island named for St Brendan lies off the east coast of Newfoundland, reminding us of his epic voyage.

A patron saint of sailors, Brendan is represented as an abbot with a boat. Churches are dedicated to him not only in Ireland and Britain, but also in coastal communities all around western Europe, and in Scandinavia and North America.

The Navigator. Bronze sculpture, 2000, by Timothy Schmalz. In front of the Church of St Brendan, San Francisco, California.

St Radegund

Born a king's daughter in Thuringia, Germany, in 518, Radegund was taken captive by the Franks when twelve and was married to the brutish Frankish King Clotaire I at the age of eighteen. After only a few years she fled this disastrous marriage (Clotaire had even murdered her brother) and founded a cloister in Poitiers. Here she lived until her death in 587, and here her body also rests today.

Radegund is portrayed as a (somewhat corpulent) queen, her robes perhaps decorated with the fleur-de-lis, and with her crown sometimes in her hand or at her feet, signifying her rejection of her royal dignity.

There lived also another St Radegund, who was a peasant girl in thirteenth-century Bavaria. She worked in Castle Wellenburg near Augsburg and cared for the lepers of a nearby leper colony. When ministering to them she was attacked by wolves and died of her wounds three days later.

These two Radegunds are sometimes conflated. For instance, the coat of arms of the Styrian village of St Radegund in Austria displays two wolves' heads, while a guide to the community claims that the village was named for a French queen and saint who was always accompanied by wolves.

St Radegund. Church of Notre-Dame and Saint-Junien, Lusignan, France.

ST KENTIGERN

Kentigern, more familiarly known by his pet name Mungo (a corruption of the Gaelic for 'darling'), was born around 518, perhaps in Lothian, Scotland. He evangelized large parts of what is today Cumbria and south-west Scotland and became the first Bishop of Strathclyde. He preached at first under an oak tree from which a bell hung to summon his congregation. One of his many legends relates how he restored a dead robin to life. Another tells how he saved the honour of the Queen of Strathclyde when at his behest a salmon retrieved from the River Clyde a ring, a gift from the King, which she had given to an admirer who, rather ungallantly, threw it into the river. The saint died around 600, and his tomb can be visited in the crypt of St Mungo's Cathedral in Glasgow.

Kentigern's story is commemorated in the coat of arms of Glasgow. Together with the bishop saint, it shows an oak with a bell and a bird, and also a fish with a ring in its mouth (with two other fish as armorial supporters). The city's original motto 'Let Glasgow flourish by the preaching of the Word' refers to Kentigern's ministry. This was later shortened to today's more pragmatic 'Let Glasgow flourish'. The city arms gave rise to the familiar Glasgow tag:

Here's the bird that never flew,
Here's the tree that never grew,
Here's the bell that never rang,
Here's the fish that never swam.

Emblems of St Kentigern (St Mungo) on a lamppost
outside St Mungo's Cathedral, Glasgow.

ST COLUMBA

A patron saint of both Ireland and Scotland, Columba (Gaelic: Columcille) was one of the outstanding figures of the Celtic Church. Born into a noble family in Gartan, Donegal, about 521, he early became a monk and a priest, but was also a noted scholar and poet. It may have been his responsibility for a battle between monasteries that occasioned his exile, voluntary or imposed, from Ireland. Whatever the cause, he came in 563 with twelve followers to the island of Iona off south-west Scotland, which he made his home until his death in 597. Here he built the abbey from which he christianized western Scotland and much of the Highlands. Iona became, indeed, a major seat of European learning (the *Book of Kells* may have been transcribed here), and from it Christian influence radiated to southern Scotland and Northumbria. Columba was also the first of a long series of Irish missionary monks who later evangelized and transformed not only the British mainland, but also considerable parts of continental Europe, from France to Switzerland, Italy, Germany and Austria. Practices introduced by him dominated churches in Ireland, Scotland and Northumbria until superseded by Roman observances after the Synod of Whitby in 664. Destroyed first by the Vikings and again in the Reformation, Iona Abbey was reconstructed in the twentieth century. As the seat of the Iona Community, it is today the centre of a vigorous and progressive ecumenical and social movement of international reach.

Like many another saint of his day, Columba became the focus of numerous legends. One tells how by the sign of the cross he banished a 'water beast' from the River Ness into the nearby lake – the earliest notice of what is known today as the Loch Ness monster! He is usually portrayed as an abbot with a dove (*columba* being Latin for 'dove') or with a boat (with which he sailed to Iona).

St Columba and St Patrick. Detail of a tapestry, twentieth century.
St Eunan's Cathedral, Letterkenny, County Donegal.

ST DAVID OF WALES

As one has come to expect with early saints, David's life as popularly known contains more fiction than fact, but is not the less interesting on that account. The patron saint of Wales, he was born and lived probably in today's Pembrokeshire,

south-west Wales, dying there in 601, or perhaps earlier. He was abbot-bishop of the monastery at Mynyw (or Menevia), nowadays St Davids, from where he founded some dozen monasteries reputed for their extreme asceticism. His shrine there became such an important goal for pilgrims in the twelfth century that two pilgrimages to St Davids counted as the equivalent of one to Rome itself.

Around 550, David was called to a synod at Brevi, Wales, where he distinguished himself by his energetic opposition to heretical trends within the Church of the day. So eloquent was his preaching, legend relates, that a little hill miraculously rose under him that he might project his voice the better.

On St David's Day, 1 March, the Welsh traditionally wear a leek or a daffodil. (Shakespeare alludes to their practice of wearing a leek in *Henry V.*) The reasons for this tradition are obscure. It has been claimed that the saint instructed the Welsh soldiers to wear leeks on their hats to distinguish them from the enemy in a battle against the Saxons. Another, more likely, explanation derives from a pun. 'Dafydd', the Welsh equivalent of David, suggests 'daffy' or daffodil, to which the leek, also a bulbous plant, bears some resemblance. 'Taffy', from Dafyyd, is a familiar name for any Welshman.

David appears as a bishop or abbot, standing on a knoll with a dove (of divine inspiration) on his shoulder, recalling his participation in the Synod of Brevi.

St David. Acrylic painting, 1986, by Virginia Broderick.
Church of St David of Wales, Richmond, California.

ST LEONARD

Though nothing certain is known about his life, Leonard was probably that sixth-century French hermit on the site of whose dwelling an abbey was built at Noblat (now Saint-Léonard-de-Noblat) near Limoges. The legendary account of his life did not appear until the eleventh century. According to this, he came from an aristocratic family, was a godson of the Frankish king Clovis and renounced all worldly wealth and honour to become a hermit and a monk. His story further relates that he devoted himself to ransoming captives, especially prisoners of war, an important function particularly at the time of the crusades, during which period he was most popular. He became the patron saint of prisoners, who on their release would sometimes hang up their chains in churches dedicated to him. Occasionally he is listed among the Fourteen Holy Helpers.

In art Leonard is represented as a monk, or an abbot with his staff, with chains or broken fetters.

St Leonard. Polychrome wood statue, 1720.
Parish Church of St Leonhard, Finkenberg, Tyrol, Austria.

ST GREGORY THE GREAT

Gregory, the first pope of that name, was one of the most powerful and influential of all the popes and was in a sense the founder of the medieval papacy. He was born of a wealthy patrician family in Rome around 540. On the death of his father, he sold much of his property, founded six monasteries in Sicily and one in Rome, and gave generously to the poor. He then became a monk himself and remained one until his election as pope in 590. He died in Rome in 604. In a period of foreign invasions and political chaos in Italy, Gregory firmly established the secular power of the Church in that country; and within the Church itself he established the authority of the papacy. He was the author of works on theology and pastoral care and of a Lives of the Saints (his *Dialogues*), as well as of sermons and many letters. Along with Jerome, Ambrose and Augustine, he is one of the four Latin Doctors of the Church.

Gregory is portrayed as a pope with a book, often writing at his desk, with a dove dictating his words, symbolic of his supposed inspiration by the holy spirit.

Remembered today not least for his part in the codification of church music, Gregory is commemorated in the Gregorian Chant, named after him, though his actual part in the development of this chant is unclear. He deserves to be better known for his role in the conversion of the Anglo-Saxons, to whom in 596 he sent Augustine (later, St Augustine of Canterbury) with forty monks as missionaries – for which reason Gregory has been called the Apostle of the English.

St Gregory. Oil on canvas by Matthias Stom (1600–1650).
Öffentliche Kunstsammlung, Basle.

ST ISIDORE THE BISHOP
& ST LEANDER

A bishop or archbishop can be recognized by his vestments in art, but is generally not further identifiable unless he displays some unique symbol or attribute. Isidore and Leander were brothers and, at different times, were both Archbishops of Seville, Spain. They can be distinguished from other archbishops by the way that they tend to appear in each other's company, usually in Spain, in which case Isidore, who was a great scholar, may carry a book and a pen.

The brothers were born of a Romano-Hispanic family originally from Cartagena in south-east Spain, Leander around 540 and Isidore around 560. As Archbishop of Seville from about 584 to 600, Leander is best remembered for his conversion to orthodoxy of many Arian West Goths, who did not acknowledge the equality of Jesus the Son with God the Father and the Holy Spirit. Isidore, immediately succeeding him, served as archbishop for another thirty-six years, until his death in 636. In this early period of the Church in Spain, he distinguished himself for ecclesiastical organization, for the construction of schools and libraries and for the education of priests. Like Leander, he also worked for the conversion of the Arians. Beyond this, Isidore was one of the outstanding intellectuals of his time. He wrote on theology, geography, astronomy and history, including an important *History of the Goths*. It has been claimed that his principal work, the *Etymologies*, represents a summing up of the entire

knowledge of his age. Isidore is a Doctor of the Church and a patron saint of Spain.

St Isidore and St Leander. Oil on canvas. Museum of Seville Cathedral.
Isidore is on the right, Leander on the left.

St Wendelin. Oil on canvas, by Michel Gessler (1850–*c*.1930).
Church of St Vitus and St Deocar, Herrieden, Bavaria.

ST WENDELIN

In portrayals, Wendelin is one of the most charmingly bucolic among the saints. Little is known about his real life apart from the fact that he lived as a hermit, later as a monk and abbot, near today's St Wendel in Saarland, Germany, where he was also buried after his death around 617. The church dedicated to him is still a destination for pilgrims today. Legend relates that Wendelin was a Scottish or Irish prince who, in his youth, stopped at this spot when returning home from a pilgrimage to Rome, and remained here as a hermit. Renouncing all claims to his father's throne, he supported himself by becoming a herdsman for a neighbouring nobleman. So impressed was this man by his herdsman's holiness that he built him a little hermitage near his castle. Wendelin was later elected abbot by the monks of the nearby Abbey of Tholey.

A patron saint of farmers and herdsmen, Wendelin is typically shown with sheep, cows and other domestic animals. The crown that he renounced may lie at his feet, while he holds in his hand either a shepherd's crook or a staff with a little scoop at the end. German shepherds use such an implement to cast pieces of soil or dirt beyond the sheep in their flock to keep them from straying. One sees pictures and statues of Wendelin quite frequently in churches in southern Germany and Saarland.

ST ETHELDREDA
(or AUDREY)

Until the Reformation, Etheldreda was the most revered Anglo-Saxon woman saint in England, and her grave at Ely was an important pilgrimage destination. She was born a princess, probably at Exning, Suffolk, about 630, and lived in two apparently chaste marriages before becoming a nun. After her first husband's early death she withdrew for a time to the Isle of Ely, part of her dowry, in East Anglia. At age twenty-five, however, she agreed to marry for political reasons the fifteen-year-old Prince Egfrith of Northumbria on condition that the marriage remain unconsummated. When after some time Egfrith determined to claim his conjugal rights, she left him and entered the nunnery at Coldingham, in what is now the Borders region of Scotland. About 673 she returned to Ely and with her own wealth founded a double monastery, becoming herself the abbess of the women's part of it. She died of plague in 679 and was buried in Ely. Today's Ely Cathedral occupies the site of her original monastery.

Etheldreda is depicted as a stately Benedictine abbess wearing a crown. She is more easily identifiable by the location of her representation, for instance at Ely Cathedral.

Etheldreda is also known as Audrey (a corruption of her name). At the annual St Audrey's Fair on the Isle of Ely, cheap jewellery and showy lace, known as St Audrey's lace, were once sold. From this derives the English adjective 'tawdry' (St Audrey), applied to a gaudy object of little worth.

St Etheldreda. Processional banner embroidered in 1910 by Dorothy Yams
and 'Ladies of the Diocese'. Ely Cathedral.

ST CUTHBERT

Cuthbert is perhaps the most popular saint of northern England. Born of uncertain parentage around 634, he first enters history as a shepherd boy in the south of Scotland before becoming a monk at Melrose in 651. Here he earned such a reputation for his missionary work, as well as for his goodness and piety, that he became prior around 661. After the Synod of Whitby, which had prescribed Roman, rather than Celtic, observances for the Church throughout England, he was in 664 appointed prior at Lindisfarne, which until then had been the seat of Celtic Christianity in Northumbria. Here, too, he was much loved for his holiness and charity, as well as for his preaching. He temporarily withdrew from his priory to spend the years 676 to 684 as a hermit on the nearby barren island of Inner Farne. Yet even here he was visited by important persons and consulted for his wisdom, and in 685, against his own wishes, he was elected Bishop of Hexham. He was able to exchange this bishopric for Lindisfarne in the same year, but just two years after his return to Lindisfarne he died on Inner Farne.

The saint's remains were removed from Lindisfarne in 875 to save them from desecration by raiding Vikings. Over a period of a hundred and twenty years they were then transported to various locations in northern England and southern Scotland before finally coming to Durham, where they now rest in the cathedral. On this protracted journey, Cuthbert's coffin was accompanied by the head of the murdered King (and Saint) Oswald that had been kept at Lindisfarne. Hence, Cuthbert may be shown in art as a bishop holding a king's crowned head. Otherwise he is depicted with otters. He acquired these as an emblem because of a story that a monk once saw two otters drying and warming the saint's feet after he had spent a night praying in the cold waters of the North Sea.

Northumbrian Saints. Stained-glass window, 2000, by Robert McCausland.
Detail showing St Cuthbert.
St Philip's Anglican Church, Vancouver, Canada.

ST KORBINIAN

Korbinian was born in Chartres, France, about 680 and died in Freising, Bavaria, between 720 and 730. He was the first Bishop of Freising, where his tomb can be seen in the cathedral today. As a bishop he played an important part in missionary work first in France and later in Bavaria, to which he came at the behest of the Duke of Bavaria.

In art Korbinian's representation refers not to his real life, but to a legend told about him. When on a pilgrimage to Rome, he was supposedly attacked by a bear that killed his mule. As punishment, he made the bear carry his pack the rest of the way to Rome. He is shown as a bishop accompanied by a bear that has a pack strapped to its back.

St Korbinian. Bronze statue, *c*.1985/1988, by Klaus Backmund.
In the Maxburgstrasse, Munich.

ST GILES

The historical Giles (Latin: Aegidius) was born in the early seventh century, reputedly in Greece, lived as a hermit and founded a monastery close to present-day Saint-Gilles, near Arles in Provence. He died around 710 or 720, and legends about him date from the tenth century. These relate how he was regularly visited in his hermitage by a hind that nourished him with her milk. One day, when pursued by a king who was hunting, the hind sought refuge with the hermit. Firing an arrow at her and following her into a thicket, the king there found her protected by Giles, who had been wounded by the arrow. On this spot, Giles's monastery was later built. Because he refused to treat his wound (the better to mortify his flesh), Giles became crippled for life. Consequently, he became a patron of cripples and beggars. A typical dedication to him as the patron saint of cripples was the church of St Giles Cripplegate in London. The High Kirk of Edinburgh, Scotland, is also dedicated to him. Though he is one of the Fourteen Holy Helpers, Giles's feast was abolished in the 1969 revision of the Roman calendar of saints.

Giles is represented in art as a hermit or an abbot, with a hind and sometimes with an arrow.

The Death of St Giles. Tempera on pine wood, 1427, by Master Thomas de Coloswar. Christian Museum, Esztergom, Hungary. (According to his legend, Giles actually survived the wound he received from the arrow.)

St Boniface. Stone statue copied after 1857 from a damaged original of 1753 by Johann Kaspar Hiernle. On Marktplatz, Mainz, Germany.

ST BONIFACE

Though known as the Apostle of Germany, Boniface (whose original name was Winfrith) was born in England (probably in Crediton, Devon) around 675. It has been claimed with some justification that he influenced continental Europe more than any other Englishman.

Boniface's early and lasting ambition was to evangelize Germany, where he first worked as a missionary in Friesland before scoring spectacular success in christianizing the Hessians. In a famous incident at Geismar in Hessen he chopped down an oak tree (sacred to the ancient Germans), which resulted in mass conversions among the pagan tribesmen, who had expected him to be struck down dead for his blasphemous act. In 732 Boniface was made archbishop with the power to consecrate bishops east of the Rhine. Subsequently he founded many abbeys and bishoprics (for instance, in Ehrfurt, Eichstätt, Büraberg and Würzburg) and in 747 established his own see in Mainz. Though a brilliant administrator, he actually resigned his see to return to missionary work. He was martyred in Dokkum, in today's Holland, when on a missionary journey to Friesland in 754.

Boniface is generally portrayed as an archbishop holding a book pierced with a dagger or sword, in reference to his having shielded himself with a book of sacred texts when he was murdered. The supposed book and dagger are kept today in the museum of Fulda Cathedral, where Boniface is also entombed.

ST WILLIAM

Duke William of Aquitaine (c. 755–812), a grandson of Charles Martell, was considered an ideal Christian knight and was one of Charlemagne's chief field commanders against the Saracens before abandoning a career of arms for religion at the age of sixty-one. After founding a Benedictine monastery at Gellone in southern France, he himself entered as a lay brother in 806 and lived there performing the humblest tasks until his death. His life is the subject of the Middle High German epic *Willehalm* (c. 1210–12) by Wolfram von Eschenbach, as well as of the twelfth-century French romances *Aliscans* and *La Chanson de Guillaume*.

William of Aquitaine may be confused with the later William of Maleval, who was probably also French by birth. After a wild life as a soldier, this William went on a pilgrimage to Rome and the Holy Land still wearing his helmet and armour. He later settled as a hermit in the desolate valley of Maleval, near Siena, Italy, dying there in 1157.

Either of these two Williams is shown as a monk in armour or a helmet.

St William of Aquitaine Receiving the Cowl. Oil on canvas, 1620, by Guercino. Pinacoteca Nazionale, Bologna.

ST EDMUND &
ST EDWARD THE CONFESSOR

Numbered among the most notable of England's royal saints are Edmund and Edward the Confessor.

Edmund was a Saxon king of East Anglia. Born in 841, he was brought up a Christian and became king around 865. During an invasion by the heathen Vikings, he was taken captive in 869. Refusing either to rule as a Danish vassal or to deny his Christian faith, he was martyred, either by being beheaded, or by being shot with arrows. He was buried in the place known today as Bury (borough) St Edmunds, though during the Reformation his body was reinterred in a grave now unknown. Edmund is shown as a crowned king with an arrow or arrows.

Edward was the second-last Anglo-Saxon king of England, living from 1003 until 1066, the year of the Battle of Hastings. The cognomen 'Confessor' indicates simply that he was canonized for his saintly life and did not die for his faith. Because he had no children (the grounds for William of Normandy's invasion of England), it was once believed that his marriage to Queen Edith had remained unconsummated. Edward was renowned for his charities, his care of the sick and other good works. He was also responsible for the construction in London of St Peter's Benedictine Abbey, today's Westminster Abbey, the site of coronations of English and, later, British monarchs. Recognizable as a king by his crown, Edward is shown holding a ring (his emblem) or giving a ring to a beggar.

The Wilton Diptych. Tempera on oak, 1395. National Gallery, London.
The painting shows Richard II with his patron saints, Edmund, Edward and John the Baptist.

ST ULRICH

Ulrich is historically important because his canonization by Pope John XV in 993 was the first recorded canonization by a pope (after 1234 papal approval became obligatory). A Bishop of Augsburg, Germany, he was born near Zürich, Switzerland, about 890 and died in Augsburg around 973.

A legend associates Ulrich with the abstention from eating meat on a Friday that was previously binding for Catholics. He was supposedly dining with a visiting churchman on a Thursday evening and the meal continued until after midnight. When a servant pointed out that they were eating meat on a Friday, the meat miraculously changed into a fish.

Ulrich is portrayed as a bishop with a fish.

St Ulrich. Plaster statue, 1874, from the Mayer workshop in Munich. Church of St Martin, Amberg, Bavaria.

There's no avoiding St Willigis in Mainz.
Here we see his emblem on a manhole cover.

ST WILLIGIS

Archbishop of Mainz, the most important see in Germany, from 975 until his death in 1011, Willigis was one of the most influential churchmen in German history. A confidant of German emperors and of popes, he was for a time chaplain and chancellor to Emperor Otto II. He built many churches and extended the power of the Church both within the German Empire and in Denmark and Sweden.

Despite his eminence, Willigis came from humble origins in Schöningen, Lower Saxony. Tradition has it that he was the son of a carter, for which reason he was sometimes mocked with the words: *'Willigis, Willigis, vergiss nicht, wer du bis'!'* ('Willigis, Willigis, don't forget who you are!') Perhaps out of defiance, he took a cartwheel as part of his episcopal coat of arms. He is portrayed as an archbishop with a cartwheel as his emblem. His wheel also appears today in the arms of the German state of Rheinland-Pfalz and, as a double wheel, in the arms of the city of Mainz.

ST OLAF

By today's standards, Olaf may appear a rather unsaintly saint. Born a pagan in 995, he went a-roving with a band of Vikings as a raw youth and had himself baptized in Normandy in 1014. Returning to Norway, he made himself ruler of the land by defeating the Danes and Swedes in 1016. He then brought in Christian missionaries and did not himself shrink from furthering their work of conversion by quite successfully bribing, intimidating and otherwise brutalizing the more recalcitrant of his subjects. These tactics made him many enemies, however, and caused him to be driven out with the help of the Anglo-Danish King Canute in 1029. While trying to regain his throne he was slain at the Battle of Stiklestad in 1030. Olaf was an unlikely holy man, indeed, yet with time he came to achieve the status of a sort of national hero-saint and became the patron of Norway. He had, of course, unified and Christianized his country, he stood for independence from Denmark and Sweden, and his death ultimately came to be regarded as martyrdom.

Olaf appears as a king slaying or trampling on a dragon, symbolic of vanquished heathendom.

St Olaf. Altar painting, 1893, by Pius Welonski.
Basilica of Santi Ambrogio e Carlo, Rome.

ST BENNO

The patron saint of Munich, south Germany's foremost city and the capital of Bavaria, Benno was actually a native of north Germany. He was born in Hildesheim, Lower Saxony, in 1010 and became Bishop of Meissen in 1066. In this period of conflict between the German emperor and the pope in Rome, Benno owed allegiance to both and frequently found his position close to untenable. He died in 1107.

A picturesque legend is told about this saint. Fearing at one point that his cathedral of Meissen might fall into the hands of the emperor's troops, he ordered its keys to be thrown into the River Elbe. When he required them again at a later date, they were miraculously recovered from the stomach of a fish caught in the river.

In 1580, during the Reformation, Benno's relics were translated from Meissen to Munich, in whose Frauenkirche they now rest. He is represented as a bishop with a fish and keys.

The canonization of Benno in 1523 provoked a denunciation of the cult of saints by Martin Luther.

St Benno. Gilt wood relief, mid eighteenth century. Old St Peter's Church, Munich. The fish and keys were added at a later date.

ST ISIDORE THE FARMER

Known for his piety and good works, Isidore was a simple farm labourer all his life. He was born in Madrid in about 1070 or 1080 and died there in 1130. Now a patron saint of Madrid and of farmers, he is especially venerated in Spain, but also in agricultural areas of other countries, in the Americas as well as in Europe. When Philip III of Spain fell gravely ill about 1615, Isidore's relics were brought to his sick room and he recovered. Philip then petitioned for his canonization. He was canonized in 1622 together with three other major Spanish saints: Ignatius Loyola, Teresa of Ávila and Francis Xavier.

Isidore is generally represented as a peasant carrying a farm implement such as a spade or a sickle. Other depictions reflect legends told of him, showing him, for example, at work in the field accompanied by angels or praying while angels do his ploughing for him. In Austria and Bavaria he is sometimes represented together with Notburga of Eben, an Austrian peasant saint.

St Isidore the Farmer. Tavern sign, Madrid.

ST BERNARD OF CLAIRVAUX

Bernard of Clairvaux was a major figure in both the Church and the public life of twelfth-century France. A member of an aristocratic family, he was born at Fontaine-les-Dijon in Burgundy around 1090. After studies at the University of Paris, he, with thirty-one others he inspired, entered the reformed Benedictine monastery at Cîteaux (Latin: Cistercium). He thus became a Cistercian. When the monastery became overcrowded, he and twelve companions moved in 1115 to Clairvaux, where as abbot he established a new Cistercian community. By the time of his death there in 1153, Clairvaux accommodated seven hundred monks and had established sixty-eight daughter houses throughout Europe.

The remarkable success of the Cistercian Order was largely attributable to Bernard's leadership qualities, organizational abilities and brilliant oratory (he is known as the Mellifluous Doctor). Unfortunately, he also employed his gifts to preach the Second Crusade, an unmitigated disaster for which he has been held at least in part responsible. (He himself blamed its catastrophic outcome on the crusaders' sinfulness.) More positively, in a display of tolerance perhaps unexpected in view of his crusading fervour, Bernard opposed persecution of the Jews and in 1146 helped put an end to a series of pogroms in the Rhineland.

Bernard left behind many influential writings, including his *Letters*, a treatise *On the Love of God* and a series of sermons *On the Song of Songs*. A story relates that in a vision he was visited by the Virgin Mary, who nourished him with her milk.

This supposedly accounted for his great eloquence. Usually, he is shown simply as a Cistercian abbot in his white habit, while as a Doctor of the Church he may hold a book.

The Saint Bernard dog does not take its name from St Bernard of Clairvaux, but from the eleventh-century St Bernard of Montjoux (or Mouthon). This earlier Bernard founded guesthouses for travellers on the Great St Bernard and Little St Bernard Passes, named for him, between Switzerland and Italy. The monks there bred their large dogs specially to track and rescue travellers lost in the snow. Bernard of Montjoux has been the patron saint of mountain climbers since 1923.

The Vision of St Bernard. Oil on canvas, c.1650, by Alonso Cano. Museo del Prado, Madrid.

ST THOMAS OF CANTERBURY
(THOMAS BECKET)

Born of a wealthy family in London in 1118, Thomas Becket was educated for a career in the Church at schools in England, France and Italy. After his father's death he worked for a time as a clerk, then entered the service of the Archbishop of Canterbury, who advanced him to the position of archdeacon and in 1155 recommended him as Lord Chancellor to the young Henry II. In this capacity he showed himself a capable administrator, diplomat and soldier, and became a bosom friend of the king. His life at this phase was that of a fashionable, self-indulgent and luxury-loving courtier, and he supported Henry in all his undertakings, even when these ran counter to the Church's interests. Assuming this sort of relationship would continue, Henry achieved Becket's election as Archbishop of Canterbury in 1162. Now ordained a priest, however, Becket unexpectedly renounced his former way of life, resigned the chancellorship and assumed with a vengeance the responsibilities of his new office. This resulted in a series of bitter disputes between the headstrong king and his now intransigent former friend. Conflict ranged over a wide spectrum of jurisdictional issues, both ecclesiastical and civil. Matters reached such a pass that Becket fled to France, where he remained for six years. In the year of his return (1170) he was murdered in his own cathedral by four of Henry's barons. This was their response to the king's query as to who would rid him of this 'turbulent priest'.

The murder of Becket was viewed with horror throughout Europe, and he was immediately regarded as a martyr in the defence of the Church against secular power. Miracles were reported at his tomb in Canterbury, and he was canonized in 1173, within three years of his death. His shrine made Canterbury one of Europe's foremost medieval pilgrimage centres, as immortalized in Chaucer's *Canterbury Tales*. The saint also inspired the dramas *Becket* by Tennyson and *Murder in the Cathedral* by T. S. Eliot. Jean Anouilh's French play was made into a much-lauded film, *Becket* (1964), with Richard Burton and Peter O'Toole.

Depictions of Thomas of Canterbury show him as an archbishop struck on the head with a sword.

St Thomas of Canterbury. Medallion relief in Portland stone, 1902–3, design attributed to John Marshall, on frieze of Westminster Cathedral, London.

ST HUGH OF LINCOLN

Born in France around 1140, Hugh had for several years been a Carthusian monk at the monastery of the Grande Chartreuse near Grenoble before being called to England by King Henry II in 1175. Henry appointed him abbot of the neglected Carthusian monastery at Witham, Somerset, originally endowed by the king as part of his penance for the murder of Thomas Becket. So successful was Hugh in administering the abbey that he was appointed bishop of the major see of Lincoln in 1186. An attractive figure today still, Hugh was fearless in his defence of the common people against unjust forest laws and in his defence of Jews, who were then subject to public abuse and persecution in many parts of England. He also began reconstruction of Lincoln Cathedral (partially destroyed in an earthquake), which ultimately resulted in the church that we know today. He died when on a visit to London in 1200.

Hugh is represented in art as a bishop with a swan (his emblem) that had been his pet at his manor house in Stow and had foreshadowed the saint's death by refusing to eat.

St Hugh. Processional banner, mid twentieth century,
by Kathleen Connor. Lincoln Cathedral.

ST DOMINIC

Born in Caleruega, Spain, around 1170, Dominic de Guzmán occupies a prominent place in Church history as the founder of one of its principal orders, the Order of Preachers (known as Dominicans). When in Languedoc, southern France, as a young priest, he was horrified at the conflict he witnessed there between Church authorities and the heretics known as the Albigensians. (Named after the city of Albi in Languedoc, the Albigensians were dualists who saw reality as an everlasting conflict between an infinitely good God and an infinitely evil Satan.) Dominic saw it as his mission to bring them and other heretics back to the Church, a conviction that led to the establishment of his order in 1216. Unlike the older Benedictine Order, the Dominicans (like their contemporaries the Franciscans) saw it as their duty to engage with and change society, rather than to retire from life. They became a leading order of teachers and missionaries, not only in Europe but also in Asia and the Americas. Dominic died in Bologna, Italy, in 1221 and is buried there in the church of San Domenico.

Dominic is represented as a Dominican monk, in black and white vestments, generally holding a book (his *Rule*) and sometimes accompanied by a black and white dog with a torch in its jaws. Before his birth his mother allegedly dreamed of a dog bearing a torch (symbolic of truth and light). More likely the dog arises from a pun – *domini canis* (suggestive of Dominicans) being Latin for 'the master's dog', in the sense of 'the Lord's watchdog'. Another of his emblems is a star, which his mother, or godmother, supposedly saw on his brow in a vision. Though the claim that Dominic introduced the devotion of the rosary has not been established, he may sometimes hold a rosary, or be shown receiving a rosary from the Virgin Mary, as in Guido Reni's painting *The Virgin Appears to St Dominic and the Mysteries of the Rosary* in San Luca, Bologna.

Although Dominic himself was reputedly a gentle soul, his order in Europe and elsewhere later played a leading part in some of the shameful atrocities committed by the Inquisition, founded shortly after his death.

Dominique, a hit song of the 1960s sung by the so-called Singing Nun, Sister Sourire, was inspired by the saint.

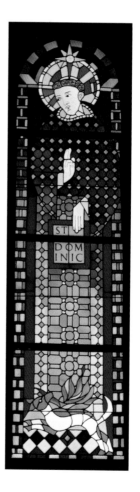

St Dominic. Stained-glass window, 2002, by David Goines. Church of St Mary Magdalene, Berkeley, California.

ST FRANCIS

Long one of the most beloved saints, Francis's appeal today still rests not least on his opposition to social norms: on his love of nature in all its manifestations and on his call to a life of simplicity and modesty. He was born the son of a wealthy Italian cloth merchant in Assisi, Umbria, in 1181. After early years of self-indulgence, he underwent a conversion that

St Francis Preaching to the Birds. Fresco, 1297–9, by Giotto di Bondone. Upper Church of San Francesco, Assisi, Italy.

expressed itself in a wish to live a life of austerity and poverty dedicated to God and to the service of the poor and sick. Disinherited by his family and regarded by many as mad, he attracted a group of followers who, like him, dressed in the coarse grey tunic of the Italian peasant. In addition to visits to Rome and the Holy Land, he travelled the Italian countryside, and he founded the religious order named, for him, Franciscans (approved in 1210). In 1223 he originated the tradition of the Christmas crib. Owing to dissension in the order about the extent to which simplicity and poverty should he practised, he was early worn out by his work and by his own harsh regime and died in Assisi in 1226.

Two main and contrasting features mark Francis's iconography. As the patron saint of ecology, he is portrayed as a Franciscan friar preaching to the birds or other animals. Analogously, he may be shown with a wolf that he is supposed to have tamed in the town of Gubbio. However, he is also depicted as an ecstatic with the stigmata – the sign of the wounds suffered by Jesus on the cross. Historically, he represents the first recorded case of stigmatization, which he experienced on Mount La Verna in the Apennines in 1224. Many artists, including Giotto, Ghirlandaio, El Greco and Jan van Eyck, have painted the scene of his stigmatization.

Francis's poetic temperament expressed itself in the words and music of hymns like his 'Canticle of the Creatures', written in the Umbrian dialect. The popular 'Prayer of St Francis' ('Lord, make me an instrument of your peace') is a modern work not attributable to the saint.

St Clare. Printed prayer card from Italy.

ST CLARE

Born in 1194, Clare was, like St Francis her contemporary, a native of Assisi, and her career also resembled his. She ran away from her wealthy family at the age of eighteen to become one of his followers and subsequently founded an order of nuns on the Franciscan model. Members of this order, the Order of St Clare (or Poor Clares), dedicated themselves to poverty, prayer, meditation and self-mortification (and today also to charitable work). Clare suffered from ill health for much of her life, and she scarcely ever left her convent in Assisi, which she governed for almost forty years until her death in 1253. She is credited with twice miraculously saving the city from the predations of the Emperor Frederick II's armies. When Assisi was under attack, she was, though sick, carried to the city walls bearing a pyx containing consecrated wafers, where-upon, the story goes, the armies withdrew. Hence, she is usually depicted as a nun bearing a pyx, or sometimes a monstrance.

Clare is the patron saint of Assisi, the Poor Clares, washer-women, embroideresses (the Poor Clares stitch vestments and altar cloths) and the blind (her name suggesting clarity or light). When bedridden and unable to attend church, she is said to have experienced a vision of the Mass – for which reason she was, curiously, in 1985 declared the patron saint of television.

With Francis, Clare figures in the popular, but overly sentimental, Zeffirelli film *Brother Sun, Sister Moon* of 1973.

ST ANTHONY OF PADUA

Anthony was born in Lisbon, Portugal, in 1195 and from an early age wished to become a missionary. He joined the Franciscan order in 1220 and was sent to Morocco, but ill health forced his return to Europe. In order to attend a general chapter of the Franciscans, he visited Assisi in 1221, when Francis was still alive. He then taught theology in Italy and travelled throughout France, and later Italy again, preaching (he was the foremost preacher of his day) and furthering the work of his order. He died near Padua in 1231. Here the Basilica del Santo was built to house his relics, and this remains an important pilgrimage site today. Anthony was canonized only eleven months after his death, the fastest canonization in Church history. For his learning and rhetorical gifts, he was in 1946 proclaimed a Doctor of the Church.

Several legends are associated with Anthony, some resembling legends about Francis. One story has him preaching so eloquently on the beach at Rimini, in Italy, that the fish stick their heads out of the sea to hear him. Statues of Anthony as a young Franciscan holding a lily (of purity) and also the infant Jesus (sometimes sitting on a book) are common in churches throughout the world. This portrayal refers to an occasion when a fellow friar believed he saw the child Jesus in the saint's presence. A nineteenth-century charity, St Anthony's Bread, dedicated to feeding the poor, is still active today, particularly in the Third World. Hence, the saint is sometimes shown distributing bread.

Anthony is popularly invoked for the recovery of lost articles – a tradition deriving from a story that a novice, having borrowed his prayer book without permission, had a frightening vision and so returned it immediately.

St Anthony of Padua. Polychrome wood statue, 1715, by Franz Fröhlich. Church of St Sixtus, Schliersee, Bavaria.

ST FERDINAND

Born near Salamanca, Spain, in 1199, Ferdinand III in 1230 united through inheritance the realms of León and Castile, thus becoming king of what is in effect today's Spanish heartland. As a specifically Christian monarch, in a task that took him over twenty years, he won back from the Moors the greater part of Andalusia, including Seville, Cordova, Cadiz, Jaén and Murcia. He also enlarged the famous University of Salamanca, rebuilt the cathedral in Burgos and converted the mosque in Seville into a cathedral. His relative enlightenment emerges through his political tolerance of both Moslems and Jews in his realm, though he did encourage their conversion. On his death in 1252 he was buried in Seville Cathedral.

Ferdinand is portrayed as a warrior king with crown and sword, standing on or holding a globe of the world. In Ferdinand's own day, of course, the world was still believed to be flat!

St Ferdinand. Polychrome stone statue, *c.* 1765, attributed to José Cortés del Valle and Manuel Romero Ortíz. Burgos Cathedral, Spain.

ST ELIZABETH OF HUNGARY

Born a Hungarian princess in 1207, Elizabeth was married at fourteen to Ludwig, Landgrave of Thuringia, Germany. From their castle of the Wartburg in Eisenach she would go down to the town to distribute alms or food to the needy and to minister to the infirm. Much criticized for this by Ludwig's courtiers, she was nevertheless supported by her husband, with whom she evidently enjoyed a happy marriage and to whom she bore three children. This all came to an end with Ludwig's sudden death in 1227 when in Italy at the outset of a crusade.

Ludwig's brother and successor ordered Elizabeth to cease squandering the family's wealth through her charities. This resulted in her self-imposed exile with her children to Marburg. Here she built a hospital, which she dedicated to St Francis, her contemporary and role model. After providing for her children, she then became a Franciscan tertiary. She died in Marburg in 1231 at the age of twenty-four, and is admired today for her Christian forbearance, for her social conscience and for the independence she displayed as a woman.

A charming legend is told about Elizabeth – the miracle of roses. Once, early in their marriage, when leaving the castle with food for the poor, she was intercepted by her husband and ordered to reveal what she was carrying in her apron. When she opened it, it was full of roses. Thus, Elizabeth is usually portrayed wearing a crown and with an apron (or basket) full of roses. Alternatively, she may carry bread or a pitcher.

Her life is commemorated in Charles Kingsley's play *The Saint's Tragedy* (1848).

St Elizabeth of Hungary. Stained-glass window, 1956.
Church of St Francis Solano, Sonoma, California.

ST ZITA

Though in her lifetime a mere servant girl, Zita as a saint possessed enough aura to inspire the Christian name for the woman who became the last Empress of Austria and Queen of Hungary. Kaiserin Zita was the wife of Karl I, who reigned from 1916 until his forced abdication in 1918.

Born the daughter of a farm labourer near Lucca, Italy, in 1218, St Zita at the age of twelve entered the service of the wealthy Luccan Fatinelli family. Despite frequently cruel treatment, she remained with them until her death in 1272. She was bullied by her mistress, insulted by her master and harassed by their children. Even her fellow servants despised her for her devoutness and conscientiousness. In the end, however, she evidently won everyone over through her kindness, modesty and sweetness of character. Outside the household, she administered to the sick and visited criminals in prison. Miracles, too, were ascribed to her, including angels baking her bread as she was at her devotions, while water in a pitcher that she intended for some pilgrims turned into wine.

Zita is depicted wearing a housemaid's clothes, often holding a pitcher or loaves or a bunch of keys. She is a patron saint of domestic servants and has been invoked especially for help in finding lost keys.

St Zita. Modern French playing card.

ST LOUIS OF FRANCE

Born in 1214, King Louis IX of France enjoyed in his own lifetime a reputation for chivalry, justice and fair dealing, and he appears to have genuinely cared for the welfare of his subjects. Many of France's great Gothic cathedrals, as well as the Sorbonne University, were founded during his reign. Like many of his contemporaries, however, Louis was also inspired by the dubious ideal of liberating the Holy Land by war from the Saracens. He absented himself from France for six years (1248–1254) on the disastrous Seventh Crusade (on which he reached the Holy Land) and he died of typhoid in Tunis, North Africa, in 1270, when *en route* to the Eighth Crusade.

In 1239 Louis acquired for France the supposed crown of thorns, to house which he constructed the Sainte-Chapelle in Paris.

Louis is represented wearing a crown, in royal robes (usually decorated with the fleur-de-lis) and bearing the crown of thorns, perhaps on a cushion.

St Louis of France. Stained-glass window, late nineteenth century, by Jules-Pierre Maumejan. Church of Saint-Jean-Baptiste, Lacq, France.

ST THOMAS AQUINAS

Thomas Aquinas, a Doctor of the Church, was an eminent teacher, theologian and philosopher who enriched medieval European learning with Classical science and thought. He is celebrated as one of the towering figures of Church history, and his ideas dominated Catholicism for seven centuries after his death. He was born the son of a count around 1225 in

Roccasecca, near Aquinas, between Rome and Naples. He joined the Dominicans as a nineteen-year-old student in Naples. This step so infuriated his father (the Dominicans were a mendicant order and hence unsuitable for his noble son) that Thomas was abducted by his two brothers and held captive at Roccasecca for fifteen months. He rejoined the Dominicans in 1245, however, studied under Albert the Great in Paris from 1245 to 1248 and then followed Albert to Cologne to complete his schooling. As an overweight and rather dour student, Thomas was called the 'dumb ox' by his fellows, to which Albert supposedly responded that this dumb ox's bellowing would one day be heard all over the world. Thomas became a teacher in some of the foremost centres of learning, in Paris, Cologne, Rome, Bologna and Pisa, and for his achievements became known as the Angelic Doctor. His principal written work, the *Summa theologica*, was, interestingly, never completed. The reason, he is said to have claimed, was that all he had written seemed to him like so much straw compared to what he had seen and what had been revealed to him.

Thomas Aquinas is portrayed as a somewhat stout Dominican with book and pen. He bears a radiant star on his breast, symbolically illuminating the Church, though legend also relates that his mother saw a bright star in the heavens at his birth. He may sometimes be shown with wings, that is, as the 'angelic doctor'.

Scene from the Life of St Thomas Aquinas. Detail from fresco, 1489–91, by Filippino Lippi. Basilica of Santa Maria sopra Minerva, Rome.

ST NICHOLAS OF TOLENTINO

Nicholas was born at Sant'Angelo in the March of Ancona, Italy, about 1245 and received his name as a tribute to St Nicholas of Myra. At the age of eighteen he became an Augustinian friar and he was ordained a priest at twenty-four. His life was spent in Tolentino, not far from his birthplace. Nicholas was an inspiring and effective preacher and is credited with the conversion of some notorious sinners. He was notable also for his dedication to the care of the sick and dying, including the criminal and destitute among them. During his own lifetime he enjoyed a reputation for wonder-working. He died in 1305.

Because of the austerity and purity of his life Nicholas is shown as an Augustinian monk (in black habit) holding a lily. A radiant star (or sun) on his breast recalls the story that a star appeared at his birth.

St Nicholas of Tolentino. Fresco, 1464–5, by Benozzo Gozzoli. Church of Sant'Agostino, San Gimignano, Tuscany.

ST NOTBURGA OF EBEN

Notburga was born about 1265 in Rattenberg and died in Rottenburg, Austria, in 1313. She was first employed as a kitchen maid to the Duke of Rattenberg, but was dismissed for giving away to beggars some leftover food intended for the pigs. She then entered the service of a farmer in the Tyrolean village of Eben. Her legend relates how once, after the church bells had rung to mark the end of the day, her employer commanded his labourers to continue working. In response, Notburga stood up, called out 'Time to stop work!' and threw her sickle into the air. The sickle remained suspended as a sign of divine approbation and has become the main motif in portrayals of her. She is entombed in Eben in an upright glass case with a sickle in her skeletal hand. One of Tyrol's most revered saints, she is the patron of farm workers, servant girls and the day's end. In rural Austria and Bavaria she is sometimes venerated together with Isidore, the Spanish peasant saint.

St Notburga. Polychrome wood statue, eighteenth century,
by an unknown Schliersee artist.
Church of St Laurentius, Rottach-Egern, Bavaria.

ST ELIZABETH OF PORTUGAL

Saintliness occasionally runs in families. Such was the case with Elizabeth of Portugal, a great-niece of St Elizabeth of Hungary, for whom she was named (though in Spain and Portugal she is known as Isabella). She was born in 1271, the daughter of King Peter III of Aragon, and was married at the age of twelve to King Denis of Portugal. A model Christian wife and queen, she patiently endured the neglect and infidelities of her wretched husband, even rearing some of his illegitimate offspring. In a more public sphere, she employed her own wealth to build or support churches, monasteries, hospitals and homes for orphans and for fallen women. She also earned the reputation of a political peacemaker, mending relations, for example, between her husband and their son Alfonso, who twice openly rebelled against him. After Denis's death, she thought of becoming a nun, but became instead a Franciscan tertiary. She died in 1336 at Estremoz, Portugal, and was buried at Coimbra.

A legend relates that once, when she was taking food in the folds of her cloak to feed the poor, her husband accosted her and ordered her to show him what she was carrying. When she opened her cloak only roses were to be seen. This story clearly echoes the miracle of roses legend of Elizabeth of Hungary. As one might expect, the two saints are similarly portrayed as crowned ladies bearing roses in the folds of their cloaks, or carrying bread or a pitcher.

St Elizabeth of Portugal. Plaster statue.
Church of Our Lady of Guadalupe, Puerto Vallarta, Mexico.

ST LOUIS OF TOULOUSE
(or OF ANJOU)

Louis of Toulouse was related to two other well-known saints, Louis of France and Elizabeth of Hungary. Born in 1274, he was the son of King Charles II of Naples and Sicily. At the age of only fourteen he was sent to Barcelona as a hostage for the release of his father, who was then a prisoner of war in the power of the King of Aragon. Louis spent the following seven years of his life as a hostage in Spain, during which time his education was entrusted to Franciscan monks. In consequence, he decided on his release to relinquish all claims to the crown of Naples and Sicily and to become a Franciscan. He entered the order in 1296 and was ordained a priest in the following year. A few days after his ordination he was made Bishop of Toulouse, an indication of the importance of power, wealth and class in ecclesiastical appointments at that time. Louis only reluctantly accepted this honour, however. He continued to live in the greatest austerity as bishop and actually resigned his position within a few months, dying soon afterwards in 1297.

Louis is depicted as a bishop with a crown at his feet, symbolizing his renunciation of royal power.

St Louis of Toulouse. Detail of ceiling fresco, 1597, by Cosimo Daddi. Church of San Lino, Volterra, Tuscany. Though the saint died when only twenty-three, the artist has endowed him with the dignity of advanced years.

ST JOHN OF NEPOMUK

John was born John Wolflin in Nepomuk, Bohemia (in today's Czech Republic), about 1345. As a priest he rose to prominence in the Bohemian Church, becoming vicar-general, or chief assistant, to the Bishop of Prague. In this capacity he clashed with King Wenceslas IV of Bohemia, first (and most likely apocryphally) for refusing to reveal to him the contents of his queen's confession. Genuine and decisive conflict, however, arose through his refusal to acquiesce in the king's confiscation of Church property and alienation of Church rights. For this in 1393 he was trussed up and thrown into the River Moldau, where he drowned. A patron of Bohemia, he is entombed in Prague's St Vitus's Cathedral.

John is represented in his priest's cassock and surplice, wearing a biretta and holding a crucifix, and generally with a halo of five stars around his head. The stars refer to a story that on the night of his murder five stars hovered over the spot where he drowned. In Bohemia and Austria statues to him are often placed by or on bridges over rivers, including a statue on the splendid Charles Bridge over the Moldau in Prague. Otherwise, John may hold a finger to his lips, symbolizing the secret of confession, as, for instance, in the ceiling fresco by Johann Jakob Zeiller and Franz Anton Zeiller in the Benedictine Abbey Church of Ottobeuren, Bavaria.

St John of Nepomuk. Stone statue, after 1729, by Claude Curé. On bridge over the River Main, Würzburg, Bavaria.

ST CATHERINE OF SIENA

One of Italy's most celebrated saints, Catherine was born in Siena in 1347 as the youngest of the more than twenty children of the Benincasa family. Refusing to comply with her parents' wishes that she should marry, she became a Dominican tertiary at the age of eighteen. She dedicated herself to the care of the sick and dying, and particularly to victims of leprosy and of the plague, which she herself caught though she survived it. In her later years she involved herself in politics and became an advisor to popes. At a crucial point when the papacy was in danger of falling under the control of the French monarchy, she was instrumental in persuading Pope Gregory XI to leave Avignon and return to Rome; and she subsequently helped Urban VI retain the papacy at the time of the Great Schism in the Church. Although she never learned to write, Catherine dictated over 380 letters, some of which are political in nature while others have become classics of mystical theology. She died in Rome in 1380, was canonized in 1461 and was declared a Doctor of the Church in 1970.

Catherine's spirituality expressed itself in mystical visions, and she is one of the notable saints to have received the stigmata. In one of her visions, as she reported, Jesus offered her the choice of an earthly crown or a crown of thorns, and she chose the crown of thorns. In another vision she saw herself mystically wed to Jesus, from whom she received a ring. Fra Bartolomeo has portrayed this scene in his *Marriage of St Catherine of Siena* in the Louvre.

The commonest portrayals of Catherine show her as a Dominican nun, with a lily (of purity), a crucifix or a book, or wearing or receiving a crown of thorns. Her hands may show the stigmata.

The Ecstasy of Catherine of Siena. Oil on canvas, 1743, by Pompeo Batoni. Museo Nazionale di Villa Guinigi, Lucca, Tuscany.

ST ROCH

Roch is an easily identifiable saint with a life story that is legendary in its most prominent features. He is said to have been born of a wealthy family in Montpellier, Provence, around 1350. Early left an orphan, he became a hermit, and then spent much of his life on pilgrimages. While in Piacenza, Italy, on a pilgrimage to Rome, he is supposed to have caught the plague and to have lain in the woods close to death. He recovered, however, thanks to the wondrous intervention of a dog that daily brought him bread. He is reputed to have later miraculously cured other victims of the plague. After returning to Montpellier, he died there about 1380.

Since Roch was invoked against pestilence, he was in the past a much venerated saint in Europe and he is included among the Fourteen Holy Helpers. Representations commonly show him as a pilgrim, with wide-brimmed hat, scallop shell and knobbed staff. He points to an open plague wound on his leg and is accompanied by a little dog carrying a roll or a loaf of bread in its jaws.

St Roch. Polychrome wood statue, 1702.
Basilica of Santa Cristina, Bolsena, Tuscany.

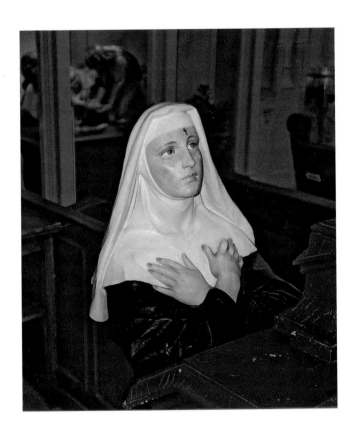

ST RITA

Rita was born around 1380 in Roccaporena, near Spoleto in Italy, and was married against her will at an early age to a violent and profligate man. Their extremely unsatisfactory marriage ended when her husband was murdered in a brawl. Her two sons thereupon swore to avenge the deed, though both of them died before they could do so. Rita then entered an Augustinian convent in Cascia, where she dedicated herself to a life of penance, prayer and meditation. Her mystical identification with the crucified Christ caused a wound to open on her brow (the mark of the crown of thorns), which remained with her for the last fifteen years of her life until she died in her convent in 1457.

Rita is portrayed as a nun in black habit with white wimple, and is clearly recognizable by the wound on her brow. She is venerated as a patron saint of desperate causes, especially in cases of marital breakdown.

St Rita. Polychrome plaster statue, *c.*1910.
National Shrine of St Francis of Assisi, San Francisco, California.

ST BERNARDINO

Bernardino was born in Massa Marittima, near Siena, Italy, in 1380. At the age of twenty-two or twenty-three he became a Franciscan and one year later was ordained a priest. After a time as a cloistered solitary, he began what turned out to be a brilliantly successful career as a mission preacher. He travelled the length and breadth of Italy, addressing enormous crowds, often outdoors, fulminating against the evils of the age (including usury, gambling and Italian inter-city warfare) and encouraging devotion to the Holy Name of Jesus, as a sort of shorthand for Jesus himself. (Alas, his sermons also exhibited hatred of the Jews and a belief in widespread witchcraft, showing that he was himself not entirely free of the evils of his age.) For a period of twelve years he served as vicar-general of his Observant branch of the Franciscan order, but resigned the position to return to preaching. He died in Aquila in 1444 while on a mission trip.

Bernardino is characteristically portrayed as a thin-faced Franciscan in his grey habit, holding a tablet displaying the letters IHS (abbreviation for Jesus in Greek) in a circle of rays. His use of this tablet as a sort of prop in preaching devotion to Jesus led to an accusation of idolatry by the Inquisition, though he was acquitted of the charge. The story is told of a printer of playing cards who complained that Bernardino's opposition to gambling had ruined his livelihood. Bernardino advised him to switch to printing cards showing the Holy Name, which supposedly made the printer's fortune!

St Bernardino. Church of San Francisco, Santiago de Compostela, Spain.
Here Bernardino holds a banner, rather than a tablet, with the Holy Name.

ST JOAN OF ARC

Joan of Arc was born to a peasant family in the village of Domrémy, Lorraine, in 1412. At this time the English, whose kings claimed French lands as part of their inheritance, occupied much of France. From her thirteenth year Joan believed she heard the voices of Michael and other saints urging her to save her country. In a period dominated by wealthy, powerful and aristocratic men, this simple girl at the age of seventeen persuaded the heir to the French throne and his advisors to let her exercise a decisive influence over the French

troops. In their midst, clad in shining armour, she freed Orleans from the English in 1429 and performed other military feats before standing by the dauphin at his coronation as Charles VII in Rheims.

Captured by the Burgundian allies of the English in 1430 and handed over by the English to the Bishop of Beauvais, Joan was tried for heresy and witchcraft. Though tempted to repudiate what her voices had told her, she found the strength to remain true to what she saw as her sacred mission and, at the age of only nineteen, she was burnt at the stake in Rouen. Her ashes were thrown into the Seine.

Joan was canonized only in 1920, a gesture that eased the restoration of strained relations between the Holy See and France. As she is now one of the patrons of France, statues to her can be seen throughout the country in public areas as well as in churches. She is represented, sometimes on horseback, in defiant or reflective pose, as a young woman in armour and bearing arms.

Joan's story has proved particularly attractive to playwrights, including Friedrich Schiller, G. B. Shaw and Jean Anouilh, and she has been portrayed on the screen numerous times, notably by Ingrid Bergman (1948), Jean Seberg (1957) and Milla Jovovich (1999). She has inspired many biographies, while poets as diverse as the rationalistic-ironic Voltaire and the romantic-heroic Robert Southey have based verse epics on her life.

St Joan of Arc. Gilt bronze statue, 1874, by Emmanuel Frémiet. Place des Pyramides, Paris.

ST IGNATIUS

Ignatius Loyola was a child of the period of the Reformation and of geographical discoveries. Living in that age, he felt an urgent need to contribute to the conversion (or reversion) of Protestant Europe to Catholicism and to carry the Catholic faith beyond the confines of Europe to Asia and America.

Born of an aristocratic Basque family at Loyola Castle in Spain in 1491, he was actually a soldier until undergoing a religious conversion in 1521. In this year, wounded at the siege of Pamplona, he passed his time reading a life of Jesus and legends of the saints that he had been given instead of the courtly romances he had requested. In the following year he wrote his *Spiritual Exercises*, which became the basis of the *Rule* for his future religious order.

When a student at the Sorbonne in Paris (1528–34), Ignatius attracted to him a group of like-thinking men, including the later missionary Francis Xavier. This became the nucleus of the Society of Jesus (Jesuits), the order that he founded and which received papal approval in 1540. The members of this order became the spearhead of the Catholic Counter-Reformation. A clear response to the Reformation can be seen, for instance, in their vow not only of chastity and poverty, but of special obedience to the pope in missions entrusted to them. Ignatius served as General of the Society from its inception until his death in Rome in 1556.

Ignatius is shown as an ascetic, black-bearded bald man in Jesuit garments (black coat with high collar) or in priestly vestments. He may hold a book (his *Rule*) in his hands and may display the monogram IHS. He is associated also with the phrase *'Ad maiorem Dei gloriam'* ('To the greater glory of God'), which is the Jesuit motto.

Historically, the Jesuits have enjoyed a chequered reputation. For their imputed political cynicism and intrigues, they have been banned from many countries at different times and were even officially abolished by the Church between 1773 and 1814. This view must be counter-balanced by the excellence of their educational institutions and by their defence of native peoples and the underprivileged against exploitation in colonial countries in the past and in many countries today.

St Ignatius. Polychrome wood statue, after 1939.
Church of the Jesuits, Toledo, Spain.

ST FRANCIS XAVIER

Born in 1506 of a noble Basque family in the castle of Xavier in Navarre, Spain, Francis Xavier has been called the greatest Christian missionary since St Paul. As a student at the University of Paris, he became a friend of Ignatius Loyola, another Spanish Basque, who with Francis and five others formed a group that later developed into the Society of Jesus.

Francis's life as a Jesuit was dedicated to missionary work in the East. In 1542 he arrived at Goa in India, which for the next, and last, ten years of his life became the base for his missionary operations. From Goa his work extended to southern India, Ceylon, the Malay Peninsula and the Molucca Islands (in today's Indonesia). His success in India was considerable among lower-caste persons, though he failed to convert many Brahmins or to achieve for himself a reasonable understanding of Indian religion. In 1549 he landed at Kagoshima on the island of Kyushu, Japan, which had only recently been discovered for Europe by the Portuguese. Here he achieved some limited success before returning to Goa again in 1551. Francis died in the following year on an island at the mouth of the Canton River on his way to evangelize China. His body was restored to Goa, where it still provides a major destination for pilgrims in the convent church of Bom Jesús.

Francis is the patron saint of Catholic foreign missions, as well as of India, Pakistan, Japan, the East Indies, Borneo and Outer Mongolia. He is portrayed as a black-bearded, usually bareheaded Jesuit in his long black gown, often in a surplice

and holding a crucifix. He may be shown, perhaps preaching or baptizing, in an exotic landscape or in the company of Asians.

St Francis Xavier Preaching. Wall painting on Japanese paper, 1949, by Luca Hasegawa. Church of St Francis Xavier, Kagoshima, Japan.

ST TERESA OF ÁVILA

Teresa was a Spanish mystic and intellectual, and the first woman to be declared a Doctor of the Church (in 1970, just one week before Catherine of Siena). She was born of an

aristocratic Castilian family in Ávila, Spain, in 1515. As a child she was somewhat wayward, strong-willed and eccentric (trying at one point to run off to Morocco with her brother to die as a martyr), and this she remained, for her adult life did not lack controversy. Teresa became a Carmelite nun at the age of twenty, but soon grew dissatisfied with the worldly life of convents in her day. Against bitter opposition, she founded a reformed Carmelite order (the Discalced, or Barefoot, Carmelites), approved in 1580 and dedicated to poverty, industry, solitude and contemplation. Learned and deeply mystical, Teresa wrote not only an *Autobiography* (1565), but also many books on prayer and letters to churchmen. Never enjoying good health, she died in 1582 worn out by hard work and by the struggle for her ideas, not least against the unreformed Carmelites.

Through her writings Teresa gave expression to her deep spiritual life. In her most celebrated visions, which she has described in her autobiography, she felt her heart pierced with an arrow of love by an angel. The sculptor Bernini has portrayed this scene most vividly. In graphic art she is more usually depicted as a Carmelite nun (with brown habit, white mantel and black cowl), often holding a book (her writings) or a heart with the letters IHS, alluding to her visions of Jesus. Other emblems of Teresa are an angel, an arrow (of love) or a dove (symbolizing her inspiration by the Holy Spirit).

The Ecstasy of St Teresa. Marble statue, 1647–52, by Gian Lorenzo Bernini. Cappella Cornaro, Church of Santa Maria della Vittoria, Rome.

ST CHARLES BORROMEO

Charles came from the distinguished Italian Borromeo family and, at a time when such connections were particularly important, especially when combined with energy and intelligence, appeared destined for success in whatever career he chose. Born in 1538 at the Castle of Arona on Lake Maggiore, he was noted for both his devoutness and his intellect as a student at the Universities of Milan and Pavia, where he earned his Doctorate in Law at the early age of twenty-two. In the following year, though not yet a priest, he was appointed cardinal, as well as chief administrator of the see of Milan, by his maternal uncle, Pope Pius IV. The fact that Charles acquiesced in such nepotism surely strikes us as ironic today, given the fact that he was to become a principal motor for reform in the Catholic Church. Fortunately, he was a man of real ability. As privy secretary to Pius, he saw to the reconvening in 1562 of the Council of Trent (1545–63), which had been suspended for ten years, and he later energetically enforced the reforms that the Council called for. To renew the spiritual life of the clergy and laity, he improved seminaries for priests and stressed the catechizing of children through Sunday schools. Sadly, his zeal also extended to using the Inquisition to root out Protestantism in northern Italy. On a more appealing level, as Archbishop of Milan (in residence since 1565, after his ordination in 1563) he spent much of his private wealth on charities. During a famine in 1570 he fed three thousand people a day for several months, and in the plague year of 1576 he went around Milan alleviating distress where he could and administering the last rites where he could not. He was known, too, as a patron of the arts, and among his protégés was the composer Palestrina. He died in Milan in 1584.

Depictions of Charles reflect portraits painted during his lifetime, for instance by Giovanni Ambrogio Figino. He appears as a cardinal in his red vestments, and is usually easily recognizable by his aquiline nose and rather unshaven look.

St Charles Borromeo. Printed prayer card from Italy.

ST JOHN OF THE CROSS

John of the Cross is one of Spain's greatest and most solemn saints. A mystic, he set down his spiritual experiences and his theological meditations on them in verse and prose. He was also a stern reformer of the Carmelite Order to which he belonged, and a supporter of Teresa of Ávila in her reform of

the Carmelite nuns. Born Juan de Yepes in Hontiveros, near Salamanca, in 1542, he joined the Carmelites in Medina del Campo at twenty-one. Recognizing his gifts, his abbot sent him to study theology at Salamanca University. Dissatisfied with the laxity he witnessed among the Carmelites, however, John soon considered transferring to the stricter Carthusian Order. He was, though, persuaded by Teresa, who had already begun her reform, to remain with the Carmelites, and in due course he founded the men's branch order of Discalced (Barefoot) Carmelites. He established the first reformed house in 1568, when he also assumed the name John of the Cross, and the Discalced were recognized as a distinct Province in 1579. Intransigence within the unreformed Carmelites had resulted in his ill treatment and imprisonment in Toledo in 1577 on the orders of the Carmelite Prior General. He barely managed to escape after nine months. From 1588 he was prior of the main Discalced house in Segovia, yet here, too, he encountered hostility. Now judged by others to be too moderate, he was forced out of office and died in 1591 in the monastery at Ubeda, Andalusia.

The depth and beauty of John's writings appeal not only to the religious, and they have become classics of Spanish literature. His poems, with corresponding commentaries by him, include *The Dark Night of the Soul*, *The Spiritual Canticle* and *The Living Flame of Love*.

In art John generally appears as a Carmelite with his emblem of a large cross.

St John of the Cross. Carmelite Convent Church, Segovia, Spain.

ST ALOYSIUS GONZAGA

The youthful Aloysius Gonzaga exemplifies an intense sort of sixteenth-century Catholic religiosity. The eldest son of the Marquis of Castiglione, from one of Italy's leading families, the handsome, charming and clever Aloysius appeared destined for a brilliant worldly career, perhaps in the army as his father hoped. Yet from his early years he was drawn to a life of self-effacement, contemplation and extreme moral (particularly sexual) propriety. Born at the Gonzaga family castle in Lombardy in 1568, he was intended to inherit not only his father's property, but also that of two wealthy branches of his mother's family. His intellectual and social education in Florence and Madrid would have fitted him, in the eyes of all, to become an ideal ruler over his estates and his dependents. Yet he determined to abdicate all his rights in favour of his younger brother (who in the event proved entirely undeserving) in order to enter the Church. Though bitterly opposed to such plans, his father might have more readily agreed had his son entered a religious order in which, through family connections, he might have rapidly risen to prominence – as did not a few of his equally favoured countrymen, such as Charles Borromeo. Aloysius, however, chose the recently founded Society of Jesus, in which such ecclesiastical advancement was discouraged. Unwillingly, his father in the end permitted him to become a Jesuit in Rome at the age of seventeen. Years of self-imposed austerities and mortifications, however, compounded by guilt at his father's displeasure, had undermined Aloysius's health. When Rome was struck by plague in 1590, he insisted on

ministering to the sick, became infected and died a year later.

Aloysius is portrayed as a pale, thin-faced, beardless young man in a Jesuit's high-necked black cassock and white surplice. His gaze is averted from the world and rests on a crucifix.

St Aloysius. Church of the Jesuits, Toledo, Spain. The head and hands of the statue, of the 1940s, are of carved wood, while the vestments are hung on a frame only. This interesting, and inexpensive, technique is called in Spanish *de vestir*.

ST MARTIN DE PORRES

Martin de Porres was born in Lima, Peru, in 1579, the illegitimate son of a Spanish nobleman and a freed black slave. In that country and at that period, he had as a non-white no prospect of ever being ordained a priest. Instead he became a Dominican brother and served in various menial capacities in his monastery in Lima. One of his assigned tasks was to sweep the floors (he is known as the 'saint with the broom'), but since he had earlier been trained as a barber-surgeon, he became known above all for ministering to the sick of all races throughout the city. His charity is reputed to have extended also to animals, including vermin, of which some charming tales are told. He died in Lima in 1639.

Now the patron saint of interracial justice, Martin was not canonized until 1962, an outcome of the modern Church's greater openness and eagerness to name more non-European and non-white saints. (Rose of Lima, of pure Spanish blood, was, by way of contrast, canonized only fifty-four years after her death.) Venerated today in Europe as well as in the Americas, he is portrayed as a dark-skinned Dominican, usually holding a broom.

St Martin de Porres. Plaster statue.
Church of Our Lady of Guadalupe, Puerto Vallarta, Mexico.

ST VINCENT DE PAUL

Vincent de Paul (1581–1660) is a saint to whom even quite ordinary people can relate, on account of the many good works that he initiated and which continue down to the present. Though he was born of peasant stock, his place of birth, Pouy in south-west France, is nowadays called Saint-Vincent-de-Paul in his honour. After entering the priesthood at nineteen, he was, according to a probably apocryphal story, captured by pirates in the Mediterranean in 1605 and spent two years as a slave in North Africa. What is certain is that sometime around 1607 he determined to devote his life to the sick and indigent, to social outcasts and to victims of war. Good social contacts, acquired through his chaplaincy to an aristocratic family, helped him finance his projects. He built schools, hospitals and orphanages and – an important need at that time – ransomed Christian slaves from the Moors in North Africa. Many goals were realized through organizations he established, such as the Congregation of the Mission (generally known as the Vincentians or Lazarists after their church of Saint Lazare in Paris). He also established a charitable organization for women, the Sisters of Charity. The important worldwide charity the Society of St Vincent de Paul was named for him when it was instituted in France in 1833. When he died he was widely venerated for his simple human goodness and his sensitivity to the needs of people of all walks of life regardless of their religious persuasion.

Vincent appears as a priest with goatee beard and in his black cassock, wearing a skull cap and with a child or children in his arms or at his feet. He inspired the French film *Monsieur*

Vincent (1948), whose screenplay was written by Jean Anouilh and Jean Bernard-Luc.

St Vincent de Paul. Polychrome wood.
Church of Santa María, Mérida, Spain.

ST JOSEPH OF COPERTINO

Popularly known as the 'flying friar', Giuseppe (Joseph) Desa was born at Copertino, near Brindisi in southern Italy, in 1603. Slow-witted and awkward as a boy, he became a servant in a Franciscan monastery at the age of seventeen and entered the order himself at Grottella at twenty-two. Of intense, indeed extreme, religiosity, he became famous, if not infamous, throughout Europe for his hours-long ecstasies and levitations; more than seventy are attributed to him. (It is recorded that, after witnessing him levitate on two separate occasions, the German Lutheran Duke of Brunswick converted to Catholicism.) He was credited also with miraculous healings and other wonders. So great was the excitement generated by such events that he was hidden away by his order for almost all of his cloistered life. He died in his monastery in Osimo in 1663.

Joseph is portrayed as a monk or priest in the act of levitating. Somewhat humorously perhaps, he has been declared the patron saint of pilots, airline travellers and astronauts.

St Joseph of Copertino. Oil on canvas.
Church of Santa Maria della Stella in the Umbrian countryside near Todi.

ST ROSE OF LIMA

Rose, canonized in 1671, was the first saint of the Americas and is the patron saint of South America and of the Philippines. She was born of Spanish parents in Lima, Peru, in 1586. Resisting her parents' wishes, she refused to marry, and instead at the age of twenty became a Dominican tertiary, living in a shed she built for herself in the garden of her family home in Lima. A recluse and a mystic, she inflicted cruel penances on herself, including wearing a crown of thorns, or spikes, which she concealed with a garland of roses lest she alarm her mother. She also identified with the afflictions of the indigent and the sick, not least among Peru's native Indians and slaves. On her death in 1617 so many people wished to pay their respects that her burial had to be postponed several times.

Though actually baptized Isabel, she was called Rose because her mother reputedly saw a rose hovering over her cradle when she was an infant, and she received the name Rose again on her confirmation. Depictions, which are common in Europe as well as in the Americas, show her as a Dominican nun wearing a crown of roses or bearing, or being offered by Jesus or angels, a bouquet or crown of roses.

St Rose of Lima. Bookmark.

ST JOHN VIANNEY

John (Jean-Marie-Baptiste) Vianney typifies a certain type of saint – the simple, even simplistic, man or woman whose naive piety, modesty, dedication and intuitive understanding of others and their problems, lie at the core of their religious self. He was born of a peasant family in Dardilly, near Lyons, France, in 1786 and, when still a shepherd boy on his father's farm, aspired to become a priest. At the age of twenty he entered a seminary, but was a remarkably poor student. After a disruption in his studies through the Napoleonic wars, he returned to his seminary and was finally ordained in 1815, his devoutness and goodness being deemed enough to compensate for his insufficient knowledge.

In 1818 John became priest at Ars-sur-Formans, an impoverished and neglected parish north of Lyons. Here 'le curé d'Ars', as he became known, served for forty years until his death in 1859. His fame derived quite simply from his outstanding success as a parish priest, so that he is today the patron saint of parish priests. He worked unceasingly to raise the level of religious life among his parishioners, and founded a school and an orphanage. His reputation as a reader of hearts and a spiritual advisor in the end attracted visitors from all over France and beyond. During his lifetime, indeed, a special ticket office had to be opened in Lyons for rail passengers bound for Ars. Though mocked by some for his gullibility (exemplified by his espousal of the dubious cause of St Philomena), for his lack of learning and for his excessive zeal and prudishness, he won the hearts of more through the depth of his faith and his personal kindness. He was reputed also to possess the gift of prophecy and to cure the sick miraculously.

Portrait statues of John Vianney show him as a small, smiling, wizened man in a priest's black cassock, white surplice and clerical collar with neckbands.

St John Vianney. Polychrome plaster statue.
Cathedral of Sainte-Marie, Bayonne, France.

St John Bosco. Stone relief. Church of Santa María Auxiliadora,
Ronda, Spain.

ST JOHN BOSCO

Generally known as Don (Father) Bosco, Giovanni Bosco was born into an impoverished peasant family in Piedmont, northern Italy, in 1815. Brought up by his widowed mother, he knew the meaning of real poverty from his earliest years. Hence, after his ordination as a priest in 1841, his energies were directed to the spiritual and material welfare of the underprivileged young. The principal scene of his work was Valdocco, a slum district of industrial Turin. Here he organized schools and workshops for working-class boys, including the delinquent and semi-delinquent, providing for their general and religious education as well as for training in various trades. He also successfully encouraged the foundation of an order of nuns to care for the education of girls. Four years before his death in Turin in 1888 he received formal approval for his Salesian Order (named after St Francis de Sales), which still pursues his social and educational mission today. The Salesians provide a broad schooling particularly for working-class or deprived boys and girls in many countries around the world.

Representations of Don Bosco, modelled on photographs, typically show him in his priest's black cassock, bareheaded, short in stature, with twinkling good-humoured eyes, and usually in the company of a boy or boys.

ST BERNADETTE

Bernadette Soubirous has had a greater impact on the pilgrimage culture of our day than any other saint of the modern age. She was born in 1844, the daughter of an impoverished miller, near Lourdes in the French Pyrenees. At the age of fourteen, at the grotto of Massabeille near Lourdes, on eighteen different occasions she experienced a vision of a beautiful lady who identified herself as Mary 'the Immaculate Conception'. She told Bernadette to have a church built on that spot and also to drink from and bathe in the waters of a spring that the girl, on 'the lady's' instructions, caused to flow in the grotto. This spring and its grotto became the site of miraculous cures that have made Lourdes, after Rome, the most popular pilgrimage centre in Europe.

A simple and frail girl, Bernadette suffered from the publicity arising from her experiences. When twenty-two she entered a convent in Nevers, where she died at the early age of thirty-five. She experienced nothing of the commercial hubbub of today's Lourdes; she was not even present in 1876 at the consecration of the Lourdes basilica. She is, however, said to be the first saint to have been photographed.

Bernadette is usually shown kneeling before a grotto in the presence of Mary, who is dressed in white and blue and may say 'I am the Immaculate Conception'. In terms of the 'politics' of her 1933 canonization, it is remarkable that her visions of 1858 would validate the dogma of the Immaculate Conception of Mary that had been promulgated by Pope Pius IX only in 1854.

Franz Werfel, an Austrian Jew who fled Nazism through France to America, vowed to write a book in honour of Bernadette if he survived. In America he published his popular novel *The Song of Bernadette* (1942), which was made into a film of the same title in 1943.

St Bernadette. Plaster grotto, *c*.1950.
Sts Peter and Paul Church, San Francisco, California.

ST TERESA OF LISIEUX

It is probably the extreme 'ordinariness' of Teresa's saintliness that accounts for her great popularity. Certainly, statues of her are among the most frequently seen in churches throughout the world today. She was born in 1873 in Alençon, Normandy, the youngest of nine children in a conservatively pious French family. After her mother's death in 1877 the family moved to Lisieux to be closer to an aunt, who helped raise the children. Following the example of two older sisters, Teresa entered the Carmelite order of nuns when she was fifteen. Though she wished to become a foreign missionary, early signs of poor health prevented this, and she had to remain in her convent at Lisieux. Under the direction of her abbess, she there wrote a spiritual autobiography, *L' Histoire d' une Âme* (*The Story of a Soul*), which achieved enormous success and has been widely translated. Through her life and in her writings she exemplified austerity, modesty, obedience and dedication to Jesus. At the core of her holiness lay a simple and loving acceptance of all of life's adversities, small and great – from the discomfort of an itch to the tuberculosis that killed her at the age of twenty-four.

Devotion to Teresa, affectionately known as the 'Little Flower', grew quickly after her death. Miracles were ascribed to her intervention, and she was canonized in 1925. In 1947 she was declared co-patroness of France, together with Joan of Arc, and in 1997 she was named a Doctor of the Church.

She is shown dressed in her Carmelite habit, with white mantle and black cowl, carrying a crucifix and a bouquet of roses. The roses commemorate her promise to 'let fall a shower of roses' and other favours from heaven after her death. Her features in the rather stereotyped images one sees of her are based on a drawing by one of her sisters.

St Teresa of Lisieux. Plaster statue.
Church of Our Lady of Guadalupe, Puerto Vallarta, Mexico.

ST PIUS OF PIETRELCINA

Undoubtedly the most sensational saint of modern times, Pius, better known as Padre Pio, was already widely and fervently venerated during his own lifetime. His cult has, however, also aroused criticism and scepticism, even within the Church, on account of its supernatural overlay. He was born Francesco Forgione in Pietrelcina, not far from Benevento in southern Italy, in 1887. Dying in 1968 at the age of eighty-one, he was canonized in 2002, in almost record time by today's standards. Statues and pictures of him are already commonly seen in churches throughout Italy, and also elsewhere.

In many respects Pio's life, as popularly known, resembles that of much earlier saints in what one can only call its more legendary features. He became a Franciscan Capuchin novice when still a boy of fifteen, joined the order at nineteen and was ordained a priest at twenty-two. The scene of his activities was his monastery of San Giovanni Rotondo, no great distance from his birthplace. Here he founded a hospital, the House for the Relief of Suffering, in 1956, and here too he acquired widespread fame as a confessor, being credited with the ability to read hearts. Beyond this, he enjoyed a reputation for working miracles – and not only for healing by touch, but for levitation, bilocation (being in two places at the same time) and other wonders. Furthermore, Pio was an ecstatic and mystic who is said to have borne the stigmata for the last fifty years of his life, the marks mysteriously disappearing at his death.

Pio is represented as a dark-eyed, bearded Capuchin in brown habit, easily distinguishable by the gloves with cut-off fingers that he wears to cover the marks of the stigmata on his hands.

St Pius. Plaster statue.
Church of Sant'Agostino, Montefalco, Umbria.

KEY

Saints whose names are *italicized* are treated fully in the main text.

The purpose of the key is to help readers identify saints from their emblems or symbols. It refers only to saints featured in this book. It is also intentionally limited in its determination of emblems for individual saints, listing only what the authors consider the commonest – that is, the most useful for identification purposes. The authors presuppose a certain acquaintance on their readers' part with the New Testament, and hence with the story of Jesus, his family, disciples, friends and followers. It would be beyond the scope of the book to refer in its narrative sections to more than some of the better known biblical stories and incidents, such as the nativity, the feeding of the five thousand, the arrest, crucifixion and resurrection of Jesus, or the travels of St Paul. Yet some knowledge of the scriptures is necessary for an identification of many paintings illustrating biblical scenes to be viewed in art galleries, museums and churches. Hence, the book generally lays less emphasis on scenes in painting than on the portrayal of saints in sculpture or in 'portraits'.

Observing the company that they keep can more readily identify many saints. For instance:

1. *Peter* and *Paul* are frequent companions, and many churches have dual dedications to them.

2. All or some of Jesus's disciples may form a group: *Andrew*, *Bartholomew*, *James Major*, *James Minor*, *John the Apostle*, Judas (not a saint), *Jude*, *Matthew*, *Matthias*, *Peter*, *Philip*, *Simon*, *Thomas*. Sometimes *Paul* is substituted for Judas or *Matthias*, who was chosen by lot to replace Judas after the crucifixion.

3. The Fourteen Holy Helpers constitute another, larger configuration, some or all of whom may be shown together. Membership in the group varies, but it may include any of the following: Acacius, *Anthony the Great*, *Barbara*, *Blaise*, *Catherine of Alexandria*, *Christopher*, Cyriacus, *Denis*, *Elmo*, *Eustace*, *George*, *Giles*, *Leonard*, *Margaret of Antioch*, *Nicholas of Myra*, Pantaleon, *Roch*, *Sebastian*, *Vitus*. The Fourteen Holy Helpers were venerated in the Middle Ages particularly in parts of Germany and were individually invoked for protection against the most serious afflictions (such as plague) or in important life situations (such as childbirth).

4. Saints with the same name may appear together – e.g., *John the Apostle*, *John the Baptist* or *John of Nepomuk*; *Teresa of Ávila* and *Teresa of Lisieux*; *Catherine of Alexandria* and *Catherine of Siena*.

5. At the annunciation, *Gabriel* appears to *Mary*.

6. The visitation shows *Mary* with her cousin *Elizabeth*.

7. The crucifixion scene brings together *Mary*, *Mary Magdalene* and *John the Apostle* (though quite often with other figures also).

8. The four evangelists: *Matthew*, *Mark*, *Luke* and *John*.

9. The four Latin Doctors of the Church: *Ambrose*, *Jerome*, *Augustine* and *Gregory*.

10. *Francis* and *Clare* (both of Assisi).

11. *Stephen* and *Laurence* (both deacons).

12. *Roch* and *Sebastian* (both invoked against the plague).

13. *Mary* and *Anne* (her mother).

14. *Anne* and *Joachim* (her husband).

15. *Isidore the Farmer* and *Notburga of Eben* (both peasant saints).

16. *Augustine* may stand close to his mother, *Monica*.

17. *Benedict* and his sister *Scholastica*.

18. The brothers (both bishops) *Isidore the Bishop* and *Leander*; the twins (both physicians) *Cosmas* and *Damian*; the brothers (both shoemakers) *Crispin* and *Crispinian*; the sisters *Justa* and *Rufina*.

19. In German churches one may see *Margaret of Antioch*, *Barbara* and *Catherine of Alexandria* together. Hence the Bavarian rhyme:

Margareta mit dem Wurm,	(Margaret with her dragon,
Barbara mit dem Turm,	Barbara with her tower,
Katharina mit dem Radl,	Catherine with her wheel,
Das sind die drei heiligen Madl.	Those are the three holy maidens.)

20. *Margaret of Antioch*, *Catherine of Alexandria*, *Barbara* and *Dorothy* together form the group known as the Virgines Capitales.

Another aid to identification may be given by the location of a statue or picture, as for example:

1. The four evangelists (*Matthew, Mark, Luke* and *John*) or their emblems (angel, lion, ox and eagle), on a church pulpit.
2. *John the Baptist*, on or near a baptismal font.
3. *John of Nepomuk*, on or near a bridge over water.
4. *Peter* and *Paul*, on or near the high altar of a church.
5. The country, city or church dedication may provide additional vital clues to the identity of a saint.

Some common objects, such as a book, a halo, a palm branch, a lily, a bishop's, archbishop's or abbot's mitre or pastoral staff, or a church held in a saint's hands are in the nature of 'generic' emblems and cannot alone identify an individual, though they may be helpful when combined with other emblems. One should look for as many clues to identification as possible. Unlike a bird or a plant, a saint's statue or picture will not fly off, or change appearance with the seasons. The style of representation may vary considerably, however – ranging from realistic, life-sized Baroque statues complete with blood-red wounds, to austere, unpainted Gothic carvings in wood or stone with just a hint of an emblem tucked away somewhere. One must take time to look carefully.

Abbess (Nun with pastoral staff): ____ with cow: *Brigid*; ____ wearing crown: *Etheldreda*; ____ with dove: *Scholastica*

Abbot (Resembles a bishop, with mitre and pastoral staff, though robes are less ornate. An abbot may sometimes carry a pastoral staff without wearing a mitre.): long-bearded ____ with T shaped staff (sometimes with pig and bell): *Anthony the Great*; long-bearded ____ in black with raven and bread, or book, or broken cup, or rod: *Benedict*; ____ in white with book or receiving milk from the Virgin: *Bernard of Clairvaux*; ____ with deer and usually arrow: *Giles*; ____ with chains: *Leonard*; ____ holding a king's crowned head: *Cuthbert*; ____ with boat: *Brendan* or *Columba*; ____ with dove: *Columba*; ____ with dove or leeks, standing on mound: *David of Wales*

Ad maiorem Dei gloriam: associated with *Ignatius* (motto of the Jesuits)

Anchor: pope with ____: *Clement*; girl with ____: *Philomena*

Angel, archangel: ____ subduing dragon, or with scales: *Michael*; ____ with *Mary* and lily: *Gabriel*; ____ with fish, and sometimes with boy and dog: *Raphael*; ____, as evangelist symbol: *Matthew*; Carmelite nun with ____: *Teresa of Ávila*; man with ____(s) in field, or ____ (s) ploughing: *Isidore the Farmer*

Animals: Franciscan with ____: *Francis*; herdsman with domestic ____ (e.g., sheep, cows): *Wendelin*

Animal skins: man dressed in ____: *John the Baptist*

Annunciation: See **Scenes**.

Apron: crowned woman with ____ of roses: *Elizabeth of Hungary* or *Elizabeth of Portugal*; young woman with ____ of flowers or fruit: *Dorothy*

Armour: winged figure wearing ____: *Michael*; young woman wearing ____: *Joan of Arc*; Roman soldier wearing ____ and with water bucket: *Florian*; Roman soldier wearing ____, with captions 'Hodie' and 'Cras': *Expeditus*; Roman soldier wearing ____, with sword or palm and long cross: *Alban*; monk in ____: *William*

Arrow(s): soldier or young man, partially nude, holding ____s or with body pierced by ____s: *Sebastian*; Carmelite nun holding ____ or with heart pierced by ____: *Teresa of Ávila*; hermit, monk or abbot, with deer, holding ____: *Giles*; princess (or maiden) holding ____(s): *Ursula*; king with ____(s): *Edmund*; bishop with heart pierced by ____: *Augustine*; girl with ____: *Philomena*

Augustinian (Monk or nun dressed in black, nun with white wimple): e.g., *Nicholas of Tolentino*, *Rita*

Axe: disciple with ____: *Matthias* or *Jude*; bishop with ____: *Boniface*

Balls of gold: bishop with three ____: *Nicholas of Myra*

Baptism: See **Scenes**.

Basket: crowned woman with ____ of bread: *Elizabeth of Hungary* or *Elizabeth of Portugal*; young woman with ____ of flowers or fruit: *Dorothy*; woman with ____ or household utensils: *Martha* or *Zita*

Bear: bishop with ____ with pack on back: *Korbinian*

Bearded man: Most male saints are

bearded, but with some it is characteristic, e.g., ___ with infant or boy Jesus: *Joseph*; ___ with keys: *Peter*; ___ with lamb: *John the Baptist*

Beehive or **bees** or **beekeeper's hat**: bishop with ___: *Ambrose*

Beggar: crippled ___ with dogs: *Lazarus*; soldier sharing cloak with ___: *Martin*; king giving ring to _____: *Edward the Confessor*; crowned woman giving bread to ___(s): *Elizabeth of Hungary* or *Elizabeth of Portugal*; Franciscan monk giving bread to ___(s): *Anthony of Padua*

Bell: hermit with ___: *Anthony the Great*; bishop with ___, tree, bird and fish: *Kentigern*

Benedictine (Abbot, monk or nun dressed in black): e.g., *Benedict, Scholastica*

Bird: ___ (eagle), as evangelist symbol: *John the Apostle*; Franciscan with ___s: *Francis*; pope with ___ (dove): *Gregory the Great*; Carmelite nun with _____ (dove): *Teresa of Ávila*; shepherd or older man with two ___s (doves): *Joachim*; Benedictine with ___ (raven): *Benedict*; Benedictine nun or abbess with ___ (dove): *Scholastica*; hermit with ___ (raven): *Anthony the Great*; abbot with _____ (dove): *Columba* or *David of Wales*; bishop with ___, tree, bell and fish: *Kentigern*

Bishop, archbishop (For practical identification purposes, generally indistinguishable. Both wear mitres and carry pastoral staffs. An abbot carries a pastoral staff, and may or may not wear a mitre.): ___ with three golden balls or bags: *Nicholas of Myra*; ___ with three boys in a tub: *Nicholas of Myra*; ___ with ship or

anchor: *Nicholas of Myra*; ___ with his own head held in his hands: *Denis*; ___ with beehive or bees: *Ambrose*; ___ holding book or writing at desk: *Augustine* or *Ambrose*; ___ near older woman in black (Monica): *Augustine*; ___ with shamrock and/or trampling on snakes: *Patrick*; ___ with book pierced by dagger or sword: *Boniface*; ___ with axe: *Boniface*; ___ with comb or crossed candles: *Blaise*; ___ with fish: *Ulrich*; ___ with dove or leeks, perhaps standing on mound: *David of Wales*; ___ with fish and keys: *Benno*; ___ with crown at feet: *Louis of Toulouse*; ___ with sword in head: *Thomas of Canterbury*; ___ with swan: *Hugh of Lincoln*; ___ with tree, bell, bird and fish: *Kentigern*; ___ with king's crowned head held in hands: *Cuthbert*; ___ with chain or fetters: *Ninian*; ___ with bear with pack on its back: *Korbinian*; ___ with cartwheel: *Willigis*; _____ with lowered sword: *Valentine*; two similar ___s, one with book/pen: *Isidore the Bishop* and *Leander*

Boat: abbot with ___: *Brendan* or *Columba*; bishop with ___ or rescuing _____: *Nicholas of Myra*; crowned princess with maidens in _____: *Ursula*; pope thrown from ___: *Clement*

Book: A book is a common generic emblem that may denote one of the gospel writers, a Doctor of the Church, the founder of a religious order, an apostle, or any saint that lived his or her life according to the gospels. For example: (older) woman with girl (*Mary*) and holding ___: *Anne*; apostle with lowered sword holding ___: *Paul*; young beardless apostle holding ___: *John the Apostle*; Franciscan with infant Jesus sitting on ___: *Anthony of Padua*; cardinal with ___: *Jerome*; penitent with ___, striking breast with stone: *Jerome*; bishop with___: *Ambrose, Augustine* or *Isidore the Bishop*; Benedictine abbot or monk with ___: *Benedict*; Benedictine nun with ___ and dove: *Scholastica*; Dominican with ___: *Dominic* or *Thomas Aquinas*; pope with ___ and dove: *Gregory the Great*; Dominican nun with ___: *Catherine of Siena*; Carmelite nun with ___: *Teresa of Ávila*; black-haired, bald Jesuit or priest with ___: *Ignatius*; bishop with ___ pierced by dagger or sword: *Boniface*; young Roman with ___: *Pancras*

Bow (actually fuller's club): disciple with long ___: *James Minor*

Boy: bishop with three ___s in a tub: *Nicholas of Myra*; ___ with or in cauldron, or with rooster: *Vitus*; priest with ___ or boys: *John Bosco* or *Vincent de Paul*; archangel with ___: *Raphael*

Bread: crowned lady giving ___ to beggars: *Elizabeth of Hungary* or *Elizabeth of Portugal*; Franciscan giving ___: *Anthony of Padua*; pilgrim receiving ___ from dog: *Roch*; servant maid with ___: *Zita* or *Martha*; Benedictine with ___ removed by raven: *Benedict*

Breasts: woman with ___ on a salver: *Agatha*

Broom: dark-skinned Dominican with ___: *Martin de Porres*; housewife with ___: *Martha*

Burning building: Roman soldier

extinguishing ___ with bucket of water: *Florian*

Bucket: Roman soldier with ___ of water extinguishing burning building: *Florian*

Candles: bishop with crossed ___: *Blaise*

Capstan: bishop with ___: *Elmo*

Captions: 'Ecce agnus Dei': *John the Baptist*; 'I am the Immaculate Conception': *Mary* with *Bernadette*; 'Ad maiorem Dei gloriam': *Ignatius*; 'Hodie' and 'Cras': *Expeditus*; 'Venite ad me et ego dabo vobis omnia bona': *Pancras*

Cardinal: old man with ___'s red hat: *Jerome*; ___dressed in red: *Charles Borromeo*

Carmelite (Nun or monk with brown habit, white mantle and black cowl): e.g., *Teresa of Ávila, Teresa of Lisieux, John of the Cross*

Carpenter: *Joseph*

Cartwheel: bishop with ___: *Willigis*

Cauldron: See *Pot*.

Chains/fetters: abbot or monk with ___: *Leonard*; bishop with ___: *Ninian*

Chalice: woman holding ___: *Barbara*

Children: woman sheltering ___ under cloak: *Mary* or *Ursula* (who wears a princess's crown); priest in black cassock and skull cap with ___: *Vincent de Paul*

Christ Child:mother with ___: *Mary*; (usually bearded) man with lily and holding ___ in arms: *Joseph*; Franciscan with lily and bearing ___, sometimes on book: *Anthony of Padua*; man with ___ on shoulder: *Christopher*

Church: A church held in a saint's hands is generally a generic symbol only, indicating that a church has been dedicated to her or him, or that she or he founded a church or abbey.

Cloak: soldier cutting ____ with sword: *Martin*; woman sheltering men, women and children under ____: *Mary*; crowned princess sheltering maidens or children under ____: *Ursula*; crowned woman with flowers in____: *Elizabeth of Hungary* or *Elizabeth of Portugal*; woman (no crown) with flowers in____; *Dorothy* (perhaps also with fruit)

Cloth: woman holding ____ (usually showing image of Jesus): *Veronica*

Club: disciple with____: *Jude*; disciple with fuller's ____ (like long bow): *James Minor*

Cobblers: *Crispin* and *Crispinian*

Comb: bishop with ____: *Blaise*

Cow: abbess with ____: *Brigid*; herdsman with ____(s): *Wendelin*

Cross: man on or with diagonal ____: *Andrew*; disciple with long ____: *Philip*; bearded prophet with long ____ with scroll: *John the Baptist*; lady with, or finding, large ____: *Helen*; Carmelite monk with large ____: *John of the Cross*; Roman soldier with ____ and captions 'Hodie' and 'Cras': *Expeditus*. See also **Crucifix**.

Crown: king wearing ____ and bearing crown of thorns: *Louis of France*; lady wearing ____ and with apron or basket of roses, or with pitcher and bread: *Elizabeth of Hungary* or *Elizabeth of Portugal*; bishop with ____ at feet: *Louis of Toulouse*; princess wearing ____ and with arrow(s), or sheltering children or maidens under her cloak: *Ursula*; abbess with ____: *Etheldreda*; king wearing ____ and holding ring or giving ring to beggar:

Edward the Confessor; queen wearing or holding ____ or with ____ at feet: *Radegund*; bishop holding ____ed king's head: *Cuthbert*; king wearing ____, with arrows: *Edmund*; shepherd with ____ at feet, with sheep, cows or other domestic animals: *Wendelin*; king with ____ holding or standing on globe: *Ferdinand*; king with ____ slaying dragon: *Olaf*

Crown of flowers: Dominican nun wearing or receiving ____ (roses): *Rose of Lima*

Crown of thorns: king with ____: *Louis of France*; Dominican nun holding or receiving ____: *Catherine of Siena*

Crucifix: Carmelite nun holding ____ and roses: *Teresa of Lisieux*; Dominican nun with ____: *Catherine of Siena*; Jesuit adoring ____: *Ignatius*; Jesuit holding ____ in exotic setting: *Francis Xavier*; priest in surplice and with halo of stars, holding up ____: *John of Nepomuk*; hunter seeing ____ between antlers of stag: *Eustace* or *Hubert*; young beardless Jesuit in surplice, with ____: *Aloysius Gonzaga*

Crucifixion: See **Scenes**.

Crucifixion instruments: woman with ____: *Mary Magdalene*

Cup: Benedictine abbot or monk with broken ____: *Benedict*; disciple holding ____ with snake or dragon: *John the Apostle*

Dagger: bishop holding book pierced by ____: *Boniface*

Dark skin: Dominican with____: *Martin de Porres*

Deer: abbot, monk or hermit with ____ : *Giles*. See also **Stag**.

Desk: old man with cardinal's hat at ____: *Jerome*; bishop at ____: *Ambrose* or *Augustine*; pope at ___: *Gregory the Great*; Carmelite nun at ___: *Teresa of Ávila*

Devil: winged figure slaying a ___: *Michael*; hermit with ___(s): *Anthony the Great*

Diagonal cross: man with, or crucified on, ___: *Andrew*

Dog: crippled beggar with ___s: *Lazarus*; Dominican with black and white ___, or with ___ with torch in its mouth: *Dominic*; pilgrim with ___ with bread roll in its mouth: *Roch*; archangel with fish, boy and ___: *Raphael*

Dominican (Abbot, monk or nun in white habit, with black cloak and hood): e.g., *Dominic, Catherine of Siena, Thomas Aquinas, Rose of Lima, Martin de Porres*

Dove: See **Bird**.

Dragon: winged figure slaying ___: *Michael*; knight slaying ___: *George*; woman with or trampling on ___: *Margaret of Antioch*; man with ___ or snake in goblet: *John the Apostle*; king slaying ___ *Olaf*

Eagle: ___, as evangelist symbol: *John the Apostle*

Ecce agnus Dei: words of *John the Baptist*

Exotic setting: Jesuit priest in ___: *Francis Xavier*

Eyes: woman with ___ on plate or stalks: *Lucy*

Farmer: ___ with farm implements or with angel(s): *Isidore the Farmer*

Farm girl: ___ with cow: *Brigid*; ___ with sickle: *Notburga of Eben*

Fetters: See **Chains**.

Finger: priest with ___ to lips: *John of Nepomuk*

Fire: Roman soldier extinguishing ___ with bucket of water: *Florian*

Fish: Franciscan with ___ looking up from water: *Francis* or *Anthony of Padua*; archangel with ___: *Raphael*; bishop with ___: *Ulrich*; bishop with ___ and keys: *Benno*; bishop with ___ with ring in its mouth: *Kentigern*

Fisherman: *Peter* or *Andrew*

Fleur-de-lis: ___ may decorate clothing of *Louis of France, Joan of Arc* or *Radegund*

Flowers: young woman with basket or apron of ___ or fruit: *Dorothy*. See also **Roses** or **Lily**.

Franciscan (Wears grey or brown habit, white rope belt with three knots, and sandals): e.g., *Francis, Anthony of Padua, Bernardino, Pius of Pietrelcina* (of Capuchin branch)

Fruit: young woman with basket or apron of ___ or flowers: *Dorothy*

Giant: ___ carrying Christ Child on shoulder: *Christopher*

Girl: woman with ___ (*Mary*), and sometimes book: *Anne*; ___ at grotto in presence of *Mary*: *Bernadette*

Globe: king standing on or holding ___: *Ferdinand*

Gloves: monk in dark brown habit wearing ___ with cut-off fingers: *Pius of Pietrelcina*

Goose: bishop with ___ or geese: *Martin*

Grapes: pope/bishop with ___: *Urban*

Grill or **gridiron**: man holding or being roasted on ___: *Laurence*

Grotto: girl in front of ___: *Bernadette* kneeling in presence of *Mary*

Hair: woman with long ___: *Mary Magdalene*; young man with long ___: *John the Apostle*

Halberd: disciple holding ___: *Matthias* or *Matthew*

Halo (A common indicator of any saint): priest with ___ of (usually) five stars: *John of Nepomuk*; woman with ___ of twelve stars: *Mary*

Hat: old man with or wearing red, wide-brimmed cardinal's ___: *Jerome*; pilgrim wearing wide-brimmed ___: *James Major* or *Roch* (*Roch* points to wound in leg)

Head: bishop holding his own ___ in hands: *Denis*; bishop holding king's crowned ___ in his hands: *Cuthbert*; ___ on platter: *John the Baptist*

Heart: woman with ___ pierced by sword(s): *Mary*; Carmelite nun with ___ pierced by arrow: *Teresa of Ávila*; Carmelite nun with ___ with letters IHS: *Teresa of Ávila*; bishop with flaming ___ or ___ pierced by arrow: *Augustine*

Helmet: monk with ___: *William*; archangel wearing ___: *Michael*

Herdsman: ___ with sheep, cows or other domestic animals: *Wendelin*

Hermit: ___ with pig or bell, or devils, or seductive woman or women: *Anthony the Great*; ___ with another hermit (St Paul the Hermit), being brought bread by a raven: *Anthony the Great*; ___ beating breast with stone: *Jerome*; ___ with deer and sometimes arrow: *Giles*

Horse: soldier on ___ subduing dragon: *George*; soldier on ___ cutting cloak with sword: *Martin*; armed struck woman on ___: *Joan of Arc*; man struck down from ___ by bolt of light(ening): *Paul*; armed man on ___ slaying Moors: *James Major*

Host: woman holding chalice with ___: *Barbara*; nun with ___ in pyx or monstrance: *Clare*

Hunter: ___ with stag with cross between antlers: *Eustace* or *Hubert*

I am the Immaculate Conception: words spoken by *Mary* when she appears to *Bernadette*

IHS: Abbreviation of Greek name for Jesus, associated especially with Jesuit *Ignatius* and Carmelite nun *Teresa of Ávila*; Franciscan displaying the letters ___: *Bernardino*

Image: See **Picture**.

Intestines: bishop whose ___ are being removed with a windlass: *Elmo*

Jar: woman with ___ or pot of unguent: *Mary Magdalene*

Jesuit (Wears plain black clerical dress with high neck, sometimes worn with white surplice.): *Ignatius*, *Francis Xavier* (especially in exotic setting), *Aloysius Gonzaga*

Jug: See **Pitcher**.

Keys: older man with ___: *Peter*; woman with ___ or household articles: *Martha*; bishop with ___ and fish: *Benno*; farm maid with ___ and sickle: *Notburga of Eben*; woman with lamb and ___: *Geneviève*; servant girl with ___: *Zita*

King: See **Crown**.

Knife: disciple with flaying ___: *Bartholomew*

Knight: ___ subduing dragon: *George*; monk with ___'s armour or helmet: *William*

Lamb: prophet with ___: *John the Baptist*; older man or shepherd with ___: *Joachim*; woman with ___: *Agnes* (may have palm of martyrdom) or *Geneviève* (may hold keys); shepherd with crown at feet, with ___(s): *Wendelin*

Last Supper: See **Scenes**.

Leeks: abbot or bishop with ___: *David of Wales*

Levitation: levitating priest or monk: *Joseph of Copertino*

Lily: Symbol of purity. May be held by or be present with many saints. The most important are: older man, usually with child Jesus: *Joseph*; winged figure in presence of Mary: *Gabriel*; Franciscan holding child Jesus (who may sit on a book): *Anthony of Padua*; Dominican monk: *Dominic* or *Thomas Aquinas*; Dominican nun: *Catherine of Siena*; Augustinian with sun or star on breast: *Nicholas of Tolentino*

Lion: (sometimes winged) ___, as evangelist symbol: *Mark*; hermit, or old man at desk, with ___: *Jerome*; two young women with ___: *Justa and Rufina*

Lips: priest with finger to___ : *John of Nepomuk*

Loaves: See **Bread**.

Milk: abbot in white receiving Virgin's ___: *Bernard of Clairvaux*

Millstone: woman with ___: *Christina of Bolsena*

Money bag/box: man with ___: *Matthew*; bishop with three ___s: *Nicholas of Myra*

Monk: ___ with armour or helmet: *William*. Otherwise see generally under **Monk or Abbot** of the various monastic orders, Benedictine, Franciscan, Dominican, Cistercian, Augustinian.

Monk or abbot in black: Usually identifies a Benedictine or Augustinian. For example: ___ with cup, or raven and bread, or rod: *Benedict*; ___ with star on breast: *Nicholas of Tolentino*; ___ with chains: *Leonard*

Monk or abbot in grey or brown: Identifies a member of one of the Franciscan orders. For example: ___ with stigmata: *Francis*; ___ with animals: *Francis*; ___ with lily and child Jesus, sometimes sitting on book: *Anthony of Padua*; ___ displaying letters IHS: *Bernardino*; ___ wearing gloves with cut-off fingers: *Pius of Pietrelcina*

Monk or abbot in white: Identifies a Cistercian, such as *Bernard of Clairvaux*.

Monstrance: nun holding ___: *Clare*

Moon: woman standing on crescent ___: *Mary*

Mortar and pestle: two men with ___: *Cosmas* and *Damian*

Musical instruments: woman with ___ (usually organ): *Cecilia*

Nativity: See **Scenes**.

Nun: Frequently seen orders of nuns: Franciscan (grey or brown habit), Carmelite (brown habit, white mantle, black cowl), Dominican (white habit, black cloak and hood) and Augustinian (black habit, with white wimple). Some examples are: Carmelite ___ with roses and crucifix: *Teresa of Lisieux*; Carmelite ___ with angel, or with book, heart with IHS, dove, or arrow piercing heart: *Teresa of Ávila*; Dominican ___ with lily or crown of thorns, or with heart, crucifix or book: *Catherine of Siena*; Dominican ___ with crown of roses or being offered roses by Jesus or angels: *Rose of Lima*; Augustinian ___ with wound or thorn in brow: *Rita*; Franciscan ___ with pyx or monstrance: *Clare*

Older woman: ___ with the child *Mary*: *Anne*; ___ greeting or embracing *Mary*: *Elizabeth*

Operation being performed:
Cosmas and *Damian*

Organ: woman with ____: *Cecilia*

Otters: abbot with ____: *Cuthbert*

Ox: (sometimes winged) ____, as evangelist symbol: *Luke*

Pairs: two bishops: *Isidore the Bishop* and *Leander*; two physicians: *Cosmas* and *Damian*; two shoemakers: *Crispin* and *Crispinian*; two young women: *Justa* and *Rufina*

Palm: The emblem of a martyred saint. May be held by many martyred saints – e.g., woman with lamb and ____: *Agnes*; woman with pincers and tooth and ____: *Apollonia*; two men in red robes with ____: *Cosmas* and *Damian*; young man in Roman tunic with____: *Alban* or *Pancras*; Roman soldier with ____: *Alban* or *Expeditus* (with banner and with captions 'Cras' and 'Hodie'); young boy with____: *Vitus*

Physicians: twin ____ usually wearing red: *Cosmas* and *Damian*

Picture of Jesus: woman with ____ on cloth: *Veronica*; disciple holding ____ and club: *Jude*

Picture of Mary: man painting ____: *Luke*

Pig: hermit or monk with ____: *Anthony the Great*

Pilgrim (Wears a wide-brimmed hat, carries a knobbed staff and displays a scallop shell): ____: *James Major*; ____ pointing to wounded leg and with dog: *Roch*

Pincers: woman with tooth held in____: *Apollonia*; woman with breasts on plate and holding ____: *Agatha*

Pitcher: servant girl with ____: *Zita*; crowned lady with ____ and/or bread: *Elizabeth of Hungary* or *Elizabeth of Portugal*

Pope (Recognizable by three-tiered crown [tiara]): ____ with dove, and may be writing: *Gregory the Great*; ____ with grapes: *Urban*; ____ with anchor: *Clement*

Pot: boy in ____, or holding pot and palm: *Vitus*; bishop with ____ with three children in it: *Nicholas of Myra*; long-haired woman with ____ (containing unguent): *Mary Magdalene*

Pottery: two young women with ____: *Justa* and *Rufina*

Priest: For example: small, wizened, bareheaded ____ in white surplice: *John Vianney*; bareheaded ____ in black cassock, with boy(s): *John Bosco*; ____ in black cassock, with skullcap and goatee beard, with children: *Vincent de Paul*

Prophet: ____ in animal skins: *John the Baptist*

Pyx: nun holding ____: *Clare*

Queen: See **Crown**.

Ring: king with ____ or giving ____ to beggar: *Edward the Confessor*; bishop with fish with ____ in its mouth: *Kentigern*; Dominican nun receiving marriage ____ from Jesus: *Catherine of Siena*

Rock: older man standing on ____: *Peter*

Rod: Benedictine abbot or monk with ____: *Benedict*

Roman: young man in ____ tunic or toga, sometimes with palm and/or sword, or with sword and cross: *Alban*; young man in ____ tunic with book and palm: *Pancras*

Roman soldier: See **Soldier**.

Rosary: Dominican with____: *Dominic*

Roses: Carmelite nun holding crucifix and ____: *Teresa of Lisieux*; Dominican nun with crown of ____ or being offered ____ by Jesus or angels: *Rose* *of Lima*; crowned lady with ___ in apron: *Elizabeth of Hungary* or *Elizabeth of Portugal*

Rooster: older man with ___: *Peter*; boy with ___: *Vitus*

Saw: carpenter with ___: *Joseph*; disciple with long ___: *Simon*

Scales: archangel with ___: *Michael*

Scallop shell: Emblem of a pilgrim. See **Pilgrim**.

Scenes: Annunciation: *Mary* and *Gabriel*; Visitation: *Mary* and *Elizabeth*; Nativity: *Mary* and *Joseph*, sometimes with Magi and/or shepherds; Flight into Egypt: *Mary* and *Joseph*; baptism of Jesus: *John the Baptist*; Last Supper: all twelve disciples (including Judas, and excluding *Matthias*, who later replaced him); Crucifixion: *Mary*, *John the Apostle*, *Mary Magdalene* and sometimes other persons

Scourge: bishop holding ___: *Ambrose*

Scroll: ___ with words 'Ecce agnus Dei': *John the Baptist*

Shamrock: bishop with ___: *Patrick*

Sheep: See **Lamb** or **Shepherd**.

Shell: Emblem of a pilgrim. See **Pilgrim**.

Shepherd: ___ with lamb or two doves: *Joachim*; ___ with sheep, cows or other domestic animals: *Wendelin*

Shepherdess: *Margaret of Antioch* or *Geneviève*

Ship: See **Boat**.

Shoemakers: *Crispin* and *Crispinian*

Sickle: man with ___: *Isidore the Farmer*; farm girl with ___: *Notburga of Eben*

Skin: man holding a knife and his own ___: *Bartholomew*

Skull: long-haired woman with ___: *Mary Magdalene*; old man or hermit with ___: *Jerome*

Snake/serpent: The serpent is a generic symbol of evil, but is traditionally associated especially with the following: woman trampling ___: *Mary*; bishop trampling ___s: *Patrick*; young beardless man with ___ in goblet: *John the Apostle*; archangel trampling on ___: *Michael*

Soldier: ___ subduing dragon: *George*; partially nude ___ pierced by arrows: *Sebastian*; Roman ___ on horse cutting cloak with sword: *Martin*; Roman ___ pouring water from bucket on to burning building: *Florian*; ___ with stag with cross between antlers: *Eustace*; Roman ___ with cross and captions 'Hodie' and 'Cras': *Expeditus*; Roman ___ with palm and/or sword, or with sword and cross: *Alban*; ___ in armour: *William*

Spear: apostle with ___: *Thomas* or *Matthew*; soldier with ___ and dragon: *George*; winged figure with ___ subduing dragon or devil: *Michael*

Square: carpenter with ___: *Joseph*; apostle with builder's ___: *Thomas*

Staff: giant with ___: *Christopher*. A knobbed staff is also an attribute of a **Pilgrim**.

Stag: man with ___ with cross between antlers: *Eustace* or *Hubert* (hunter)

Star: Dominican with ___ above head: *Dominic*; Augustinian with radiant ___ on breast: *Nicholas of Tolentino*; woman with halo of (usually twelve) ___s: *Mary*; priest with halo of (usually five) ___s: *John of Nepomuk*; Dominican with radiant ___ on breast: *Thomas Aquinas*

Steer: See **Ox**.

Stigmata: Franciscan with ___:

Francis; Dominican nun with ___:
Catherine of Siena

Stone: man holding ___(s): *Stephen*;
hermit striking breast with a ___:
Jerome. See also **Millstone**.

Sun: Augustinian with ___ on breast:
Nicholas of Tolentino

Surplice: priest in ___ holding up
crucifix and with halo of (usually
five) stars: *John of Nepomuk*; young
Jesuit in ___ with crucifix: *Aloysius
Gonzaga*; small, wizened priest in
___: *John Vianney*

Swan: bishop with ___: *Hugh of
Lincoln*

Sword: woman with breast pierced by
___(s): *Mary*; winged figure with
flaming ___: *Michael* or *Gabriel*;
apostle with lowered ___: *Paul* or
Matthew; woman (usually with tower)
holding ___: *Barbara*; woman
(usually with wheel) holding ___:
Catherine of Alexandria; soldier cutting
cloak with ___: *Martin*; bishop with
book pierced with ___: *Boniface*;
archbishop with ___ in head; *Thomas
of Canterbury*; bishop with lowered
___: *Valentine*; Roman soldier with
___ and cross: *Alban*; king with ___
slaying dragon: *Olaf*; king with ___
standing on or holding globe:
Ferdinand

Thorn: Augustinian nun with ___ in
brow: *Rita*

Tooth: woman holding ___ in
pincers: *Apollonia*

Torch: Dominican with dog holding
flaming ___ in jaws: *Dominic*

Torture instruments: woman with
___ of the crucifixion: *Mary
Magdalene*

Tower: woman with ___ (often with
three windows): *Barbara*; two young

women with church ___: *Justa* and
Rufina

Tree: man pierced with arrows and
tied to ___: *Sebastian*; bishop with
___, bird, bell and fish: *Kentigern*

Tub: See **Pot**.

Vat: See **Pot**.

Water bucket: Roman soldier with
___ extinguishing fire: *Florian*

Wheel: woman with (sometimes
broken) ___: *Catherine of Alexandria*;
bishop with cart ___: *Willigis*

Wilderness setting: Indicates a
prophet like *John the Baptist* or a
hermit like *Anthony the Great*

Windlass: bishop with ___: *Elmo*

Wolf: Franciscan with ___: *Francis*;
___, emblem of *Radegund*

Words: See **Captions**.

Wound: pilgrim pointing to ___ in
leg: *Roch*; Augustinian nun with ___
in brow: *Rita*

Writing: pope ___: *Gregory the Great*;
bishop ___: *Ambrose* or *Augustine*; old
man or hermit or cardinal ___:
Jerome; nun ___: *Teresa of Ávila*

SELECT BIBLIOGRAPHY

The Book of Saints. A Comprehensive Biographical Dictionary. 7th edn., revised and reset. Ed. by Dom Basil Watkins, OSB, on behalf of the Benedictine monks of St Augustine's Abbey, Ramsgate. London: A. and C. Black, 2002.

Butler's Lives of the Saints. 4 vols. Ed., revised and supplemented by Herbert J. Thurston and Donald Attwater. Westminster, Maryland: Christian Classics, 1981.

Chadwick, Owen. *A History of Christianity*. London: Weidenfeld and Nicholson, 1995.

Clarke, C.P.S. *Everyman's Book of Saints*. Oxford: A.R. Mowbray, 1933.

Delaney, John J. *Dictionary of Saints*. New York: Doubleday, 1980.

Delehaye, Hippolyte. *The Legends of the Saints*. New York: Fordham University Press, 1962.

Dwyer, John C. *Church History. Twenty Centuries of Catholic Christianity*. New York: Paulist Press, 1998.

Farmer, David Hugh. *The Oxford Dictionary of Saints*. 5th edition. Oxford and New York: Oxford University Press, 2003.

Green, Vivian. *A New History of Christianity*. New York: Continuum, 1996.

Giorgi, Rosa. *Saints in Art*. Translated from the Italian by Thomas Michael Hartmann. Los Angeles: The John Paul Getty Museum, 2003.

Guiley, Rosemary Ellen. *The Encyclopedia of Saints*. New York: Facts on File, 2001.

Internet resources. Countless related sites are accessible through the Internet, but they must be used with discretion. Most useful are:
   New Catholic Dictionary, 1910 edition (http://www.catholicforum.com); and
   Catholic Encyclopedia, 1913 edition (http://www.newadvent.org).

Johnson, Paul. *A History of Christianity*. New York: Athenaeum, 1976.

Lanzi, Fernando and Gioia. *Saints and Their Symbols. Recognizing Saints in Art and in Popular Images*. Translated from the Italian by Matthew J. O'Connell. Collegeville, Minnesota: The Liturgical Press, 2004.

Lexikon der christlichen Ikonographie. 8 vols. Ed. Engelbert Kirschbaum, Wolfgang Braunfels et al. Rome, Freiburg, Basel, Vienna: Herder, 1968–1976.

McBrien, Richard P. *Lives of the Saints. From Mary and St Francis of Assisi to John XXIII and Mother Teresa*. San Francisco: Harper, 2001.

McGinley, Phyllis. *Saint-Watching*. New York: Viking Press, 1969.

McManners, John (ed.). *The Oxford Illustrated History of Christianity*. Oxford and New York: Oxford University Press, 1990.

Metford, J.C.J. *Dictionary of Christian Lore and Legend*. London: Thames and Hudson, 1983.

Murray, Peter and Linda. *A Dictionary of Christian Art*. Oxford: Oxford University Press, 2004.

The New Testament. In any edition, an indispensable guide to the stories of the biblical saints.

Roeder, Helen. *Saints and their Attributes. With a Guide to Localities and Patronage*. London: Longmans, Green, 1955.

The Roman Martyrology. Ed. J.B. O'Connell. Westminster, Maryland: Newman Press, 1962.

Schauber, Vera and Hanns Michael Schindler. *Heilige und Namenspatrone im Jahreslauf*. Augsburg: Pattloch Verlag, 1999.

de Voragine, Jacobus. *The Golden Legend*. New York: Arno Press, 1969.

Wimmer, Otto. *Kennzeichen und Attribute der Heiligen*. Revised and enlarged by Barbara Knoflach-Zingerle. Vienna and Innsbruck: Tyrolia-Verlag, 2000.

Woodward, Kenneth L. *Making Saints. How the Catholic Church Determines Who Becomes a Saint, Who Doesn't, and Why*. New York: Simon and Schuster, 1990.

INDEX OF SAINTS

Numbers indicating illustrations are in **bold**.